Baking with Fruit

Cakes, Pies and more besides

© Naumann & Göbel Verlagsgesellschaft mbH, a subsidiary of
VEMAG Verlags- und Medien Aktiengesellschaft, Cologne
www.apollo-intermedia.de

Complete production: Naumann & Göbel Verlagsgesellschaft mbH, Cologne
Printed in Germany

ISBN 3-625-11089-X

Baking with Fruit

Cakes, Pies and more besides

NAUMANN & GÖBEL

Contents

Baking Utensils

Info, tips and tricks about baking

A vital ingredient to baking and of great assistance around the kitchen is the right equipment. You don't have to have everything to make most of our recipes with but for those of you who are keen cake bakers the following can be of great help. Investing in expensive equipment should be well considered however because it is only worth it if you really intend to bake on a regular basis. Be aware also of the differing qualities in the vast range of baking utensils on offer. You will find that investing more money in a utensil will pay itself off after you have used it several times. The following is a list and description of the most important pieces of equipment for cake making.

Baking tins

Baking tins, moulds and dishes come in a large variety of shapes and materials e.g. light tin, heavy tin, copper, porcelain etc. The most sturdy are made of aluminium. They transmit heat the best and evenly allowing the cake to bake right through. They are also very easy to clean.

Bowls

Different sized bowls are nearly always needed and have many different kinds of uses, e.g. to stir a dough mixture together or to beat some eggs. For hygienic reasons it is recommended that you use stainless steel ones.

Cake cooler

A cake cooler or rack is very useful and as the name suggests allows the cake to cool down after removal from the oven. It will cool quickly and more importantly evenly from all sides.

Egg-timer

If you don't have a built in timer in your cooker then an egg timer is irreplaceable. This will prevent you from burning your well-prepared baked goodies.

Electrical Hand-Mixer

The electrical hand mixer or blender is one of the most important pieces of equipment for baking. With the right range of accessories they can be used to mix ingredients knead dough and beat egg white etc. As mentioned this is a worthwhile investment if you bake on a regular basis. They can perform at a high level and are very versatile.

Greaseproof paper

You can find it in most well stocked supermarkets and we highly recommend that you use it. Greaseproof paper allows you to work without making a mess and prevents your cakes from sticking unnecessarily to trays and moulds. It also cuts out having to grease all of your baking tins. If however you are using any pie dishes smearing butter additionally to the edges helps to maintain the form of your baked product.

Icing bag

With all the included attachments an icing bag allows you to have some fun decorating and opens up many creative possibilities.

Rolling pin

A rolling pin is very useful as an all-round piece of equipment in the kitchen and particularly beneficial for baking. You could go for a luxury model with ball bearings, but the standard models are just as good.

Sieve

A sieve should be well made and out of stainless (non-rusting) steel. They are light in weight and easy to clean. They are available in different sizes and very useful for baking and much more besides.

Weighing scales

Accurate work goes hand in hand with successful baking. The relative quantities of the ingredients can be accurately weighed out with the help of a set of scales. If you do not have any scales a measuring vase can be of great help. Bear in mind however that this is not very accurate.

Whisk

A good whisk should again be made from stainless steel and flexible to the touch.

Wooden skewers

Wooden skewers are very useful for making tests to see if the cake mixtures are fully cooked through. Simply poke them into the dough mixture towards the end of the baking time – if no little bits of dough stick to the skewer then the cake is ready.

Info, tips and tricks about baking

In our world of ready-made products and fast food, it still remains the pride of many a host or hostess to be able to present a home baked cake mastered by their own hands.

Many cooking aids are available these days and are an enormous help around the kitchen and thereby prevent any hindrances or frustration that could otherwise occur when baking. An electric blender, for example cuts out the painstaking kneading work that is often required for a good dough mixture. Ready-made pastry and baking mixtures don't even have to be kneaded and save not only energy but also time. High-tech ovens distribute the heat evenly allowing your mixtures to rise well and unfold to become delicious creations.

You will be amazed how very simple it really is to successfully bake a cake well enough to present on your table. One thing however that goes hand in hand with success is working as accurately as possible. Successful baking depends very much on using the right measured proportions of the ingredients. That is why all ingredients should be accurately weighed. Adding the ingredients in the right order is also very decisive. One aspect, however that you can treat more loosely in connection to all of the listed recipes is the given baking time. Only an average time can be quoted here because each oven varies from one to the other.

It is however easy to tell when your cake is ready by simply poking it with a knitting needle or wooden skewer. When no more bits of dough stick to the skewer then it is ready. You shouldn't do this too often however because every time you open the oven door a lot of heat is lost and this could lead to uneven baking.

The following lists useful tips and tricks that will help you achieve optimal results with our recipes and ensure when you're baking with fruit that the cakes turn out really tasty!

Eggs

Always use medium sized eggs for baking unless otherwise stated in the recipe. Eggs should be stored with the pointed end downwards and the rounded end with the air sac in it pointing upwards. Eggs are known for absorbing surroundings smells so they are best stored separately.

Raisins

Raisins will only sink into cake dough when they have been previously dipped in flour.

Almonds

Chopped almonds are a favourite ingredient often used in baking. You can buy them ready chopped or whole. If you want to do it yourself a clever way is to chop them together with brown sugar. This prevents pieces of almond flying

around the chopping board or kitchen uncontrollably.

Flaky pastry

Ready-made flaky pastry can be made to start flaking beforehand simply by brushing the defrosted strips with melted butter instead of water. Leave however a border of 1 cm unbrushed, so that the

butter does not run out over the sides, which could otherwise prevent the pastry from rising.

Steam

Cream puffs will rise better and produce a lighter pastry if you steam them while baking. This can be achieved by placing an oven-proof bowl of water in the oven.

Cream cheese

Ricotta and Mascarpone have become popular particularly in home baking and are cream cheeses originating from Italy. Ricotta is made from either cow's or sheep's milk and is available sweet or salty. Mascarpone on the other hand is only made from cow's milk with an extra shot of cream added and is always sweet. It also has a more creamy consistency than the Ricotta, which has a bit more bite.

Macadamia nuts

Macadamia nuts have a unique fine aroma and are solely available in the shops ready shelled. The shell being so hard that it can only be cracked with industrial machines. They grow in Africa, Australia and Hawaii. The large hazelnut like kernel got its name from a certain Doctor MacAdam who discovered them in the Australian bush. How he opened them is anybodies guess!

Yeast

Yeast will keep longest when stored in an airtight container in the fridge. You can even freeze it to always have in reserve. Once defrosted it will have a liquid consistency, but does not lose its quality. Badly stored yeast will turn brown and develop cracks and become dry. It will also lose a lot of its rising potential as a result.

Yeast dough

Yeast dough can be kept ready for baking when well stored. Frozen it will keep for at least 3 months. Make sure however that you only add to it half of the yeast given in the recipe and a little sugar. Let the dough rise a little before freezing and when you come to using it and after it has been defrosted allow to rise some more.

Walnut Kernels

Pre-shelled walnut kernels tend to be slightly rancid in taste. Sugar-coated walnut pieces on the other hand will stay fresh and crunchy for longer periods.

Short-crust pastry

Short-crust pastry should be left to stand for a little while after preparation. Leave it in a cool place or ideally wrapped in cling film and placed in the fridge. An additional tip is if you stir in some egg yolk and 1–2 teaspoons of

chopped almonds. This will lend the short-crust pastry a soft and light texture.

Springforms

A springform baking tin has a releasable ring and a base that is loose and it allows you to remove the cake easily for cooling and serving. They are particularly practical for baking fruit tarts.

Even a small household can create their own baked products and not have to make do with the same old ready-made stuff, thanks to the large range of special baking tins available at reasonable prices in most shops.

Fruit

Fruits do not in themselves always have the same quality. After a predominantly sunny summer fruit is usually full-bodied, round and juicy. After long periods of rain, however fruit will grow to be much more watery, and particularly affected are pears and plums. Test the fruit before using it to bake with to prevent the cake

from becoming soggy. A good idea is to include a soaking up layer into the cake. You can do this by adding breadcrumbs, a crushed rusk biscuit or coconut flakes, thereby stopping the cake from retaining too much liquid.

Butter

Cake dough does not react well at all to cold butter. Either leave it to stand at room temperature shortly before using, or place covered in a microwave and warm up briefly.

Succulent Fruit Cakes

Apples, pears, quinces, and more –
delicious baking made with seeded fruits.

Pear and Grape Cream Meringues

FOR 8 SERVINGS:

3 egg whites
A pinch of salt
100 g/3$^1/_2$ oz icing sugar
1 tbsp lemon juice
50 g/1$^3/_4$ oz dark chocolate coating
300 g/10$^1/_2$ oz pears
100 g/4 oz green seedless grapes
2 cl/$^1/_2$ tsp Grappa
6 leaves white gelatine
250 g/9 oz whipping cream
150 g/5 oz yoghurt
125 g/$^1/_2$ oz sugar
Grated rind of 1 untreated lemon
Grapes, to garnish

1. Mix the egg white with the salt and whisk until it is stiff. Sift over the icing sugar and gradually stir in together with the lemon juice. Preheat the oven to 180 °C/355 °F/ gas mark 4.

2. Continue whisking until the sugar has completely dissolved and the mixture is stiff and shiny.

3. Cover two baking trays with greaseproof paper. Make 8 bases using an icing bag filled with the egg mixture and squirting out into small rectangles. Then make 8 lids to go on top of the completed meringue. Place them on the middle shelf of the oven and bake for approx. 20 minutes.

4. Dissolve the chocolate coating, brush half of the mixture onto the base of the rectangles and leave to harden.

5. Wash and dry the pears then peel, cut in half, remove cores and chop into pieces. Wash the grapes and then mix together with the pears and boil in a saucepan until softened. Liquidise and stir in the Grappa last.

6. Soak the gelatine in cold water. Whisk the cream until it is stiff and mix in the fruit purée, yoghurt, sugar and lemon rind. Dissolve the gelatine and stir in some of the cream mixture to make a paste, then gradually add the rest. Fill the meringue bases with swirls of the fruit cream filling , cover with the lids and decorate with the remaining chocolate coating and grapes.

Preparation time: approx. 50 minutes
Per serving: approx. 222 kcal/936 kj
3.5 g P, 10 g F, 25g C

Step 3

14

Apple Slices with Cream

FOR 12 SERVINGS:

100 g/3½ oz soft butter

100 g/3½ oz sugar

1 tbsp vanilla sugar

A pinch of salt

100 g/3½ oz marzipan paste

3 eggs

150 g/5 oz plain wheat flour

50 g/1¾ oz cornflour

2 tsp baking powder

4 tbsp cream

Butter, to grease baking tin

800 g/1 lb 12 oz apples

½ tsp cinnamon powder

1. Mix the butter with 80 g/2 ¾ oz of the sugar, adding the vanilla sugar, salt and eggs, crumble in the marzipan and stir well.

2. Mix together the flour, cornflour and baking powder. Stir gradually into the butter mix together with the cream. Grease a 26 cm/10 in springform baking tin with butter.

3. Turn the dough into the prepared baking tin. Wash and peel the apples, cut in half and remove the cores. Score the surface of each half with a knife. Preheat the oven to 180 °C/355 °F/gas mark 4.

4. Mix the cinnamon and remaining sugar together. Roll the apple halves in this and then gently press and turn them into the dough.

5. Place on the middle shelf of the oven and bake for 45 minutes.

Preparation time: approx. 1 hour
Per serving: approx. 255 kcal/1073 kj
4 g P, 13 g F, 26g C

Grandma's Pear Cake

FOR 24 SERVINGS:

300 g/10½ oz plain wheat flour

200 g/7 oz butter, chopped

100 g/3½ oz sugar

A pinch of salt

¼ tsp grated rind of 1 untreated lemon

1 egg

1 kg/2 lbs 3 oz pears

2 tbsp lemon juice

50 g/1¾ oz sugar

1 tbsp vanilla sugar

200 g/7 oz marzipan paste

250 g/9 oz cheese slices

200 ml/7 fl oz sour cream

1 egg yolk

1. Add the flour, butter pieces, sugar, salt, lemon rind, and egg together to a clean working surface and chop up finely. Knead the mixture together and roll into a ball. Wrap in cling film and leave to stand in a cool place for approx. 1 hour. Preheat the oven to 200 °C/ 355 °F/gas mark 4.

2. Peel the pears cut in half and remove the cores, cut into wedges and sprinkle with the lemon juice. Mix the sugar together with the vanilla sugar and dip the pear wedges into this.

3. Roll the dough onto a baking tray prepared with greaseproof paper. Cover with overlapping pear wedges. Place on the middle shelf of the oven and bake for 10 minutes.

4. Liquidise the marzipan with the cheese slices, sour cream and egg yolk. Spread onto the cake and place back on the middle shelf of the oven and bake for 30 minutes.

Preparation time: approx. 45 minutes (excluding standing time)
Per serving: approx. 229 kcal/932 kj, 4 g P, 13 g F, 21 g C

Calvados Danish Pastry

FOR 8 SERVINGS:

200 g/7 oz flaky pastry

Butter, to grease the baking tin

370 g/13 oz cocktail apples (preserve)

100 ml/4 fl oz Calvados

50 g/1 3/4 oz marzipan paste

2 egg yolks

200 g/7 oz sour cream

3 tsp cornflour

Milk, to brush

4 tbsp lemon marmalade

4 tbsp hazelnut flakes

1. Roll out the flaky pastry generously onto a flour-covered working surface. Grease two 18 cm/ 7 3/4 in baking tins and line them with the pastry leaving the excess dough to hang over the sides.

2. Wash and peel the apples, cut into wedges and sprinkle with the Calvados.

3. Crumble the marzipan and stir the egg yolk into it. Add the sour cream and the cornflour. Preheat the oven to 180 °C/355 °F/gas mark 4.

4. Disperse the apple wedges over the dough and cover them with the marzipan. Fold the excess dough inwards and brush over with the milk.

5. Place the filled baking tins into the oven on the middle shelf and bake for approx. 30 minutes.

6. Stir the hazelnut flakes into the lemon marmalade and brush over the warm pastry.

Preparation time: approx. 45 minutes
Per serving: approx. 396 kcal/1664 kj,
5 g P, 21 g F, 41 g C

Step 3

Delicate Grape Tart

FOR 12 SERVINGS:

100 g/3½ oz soft butter

160 g/5½ oz sugar

4 eggs

2 tsp baking powder

100 g/3½ oz plain wheat flour

A pinch of salt

100 g/3½ oz ground walnuts

Butter, to grease the pie dish

200 g/7 oz green grapes

200 g/7 oz black grapes

200 g/7 oz crème fraîche

2 tbsp vanilla pudding powder

1 tbsp vanilla sugar

Grated rind of a lime

1. Cream the butter with 100 g/ 3½ oz of the sugar in a bowl until light and fluffy. Stir in two of the eggs. Preheat the oven to 200 °C/ 390 °F/gas mark 6.

2. Mix the baking powder together with the flour, salt and ground walnuts and fold into the butter mix. Take a 28 cm/11 in pie dish and grease it with some butter.

3. Line the baking tin with the dough mix and pre-bake in the oven on the middle shelf of the oven for approx. 15 minutes.

4. Wash and dry the grapes, cut in half and remove any seeds. Then place them on the dough in circles.

5. Stir together the remaining sugar and eggs with the crème fraîche, custard powder, vanilla sugar, and lime rind.

6. Brush the resulting cream mix onto the grapes and then bake for a further 30 minutes on the middle shelf.

Preparation time: approx. 1 hour
Per serving: approx. 309 kcal/1300 kj,
5 g P, 18 g F, 27 g C

Preparation time: approx. 50 minutes
Per serving: approx. 490 kcal/2060 kj,
5,5 g P, 24 g F, 56 g C

18

Apple and Quince Strudel

FOR 8 SERVINGS:

280 g/10 oz plain wheat flour

200 g/7 oz butter

50 g/1³/₄ oz icing sugar

A pinch of salt

2 egg yolks

2 tbsp milk

2 tbsp white wine

500 g/1 lb 2 oz apples

500 g/1 lb 2 oz quinces

100 g/3³/₄ oz sugar

¹/₂ tsp cinnamon

50 g/1³/₄ oz raisins

1 egg white

1. Combine the butter, icing sugar, salt, egg yolk, milk and white wine with the flour and knead into a soft dough. Roll into a ball, wrap in cling film, leave to stand in a cool place for an hour.

2. Peel the apples, cut in half removing the cores and then slice into wedges. Peel the quinces, and also cut in half removing the cores and slice into thin wedges.

3. Mix the fruit together with the sugar, cinnamon and raisins and leave to draw. Preheat the oven to 180 °C/355 °F/gas mark 4.

4. Roll the dough out onto a flour-covered working surface and into a rectangle 40 x 25 cm/16 x 10 in, trimming the edges straight.

5. Pour the apple filling onto the middle of the dough and then spread it out evenly. Take one side of the dough and fold it over the filling, brush with the egg white to stick it together and tuck neatly underneath the opposite side to create a roll.

6. Take the leftovers of the dough and cut into shapes to decorate the top of the strudel.

7. Brush the dough with the remaining egg white and place on the middle shelf of the preheated oven baking for approx. 15 minutes. Turn the oven down to 160 °C/320 °F/gas mark 2–3 and bake for about a further 25 minutes.

Yoghurt Flat Cakes

FOR 6 SERVINGS:

50 g/1³/₄ oz butter

50 g/1³/₄ oz icing sugar

1 egg white

50 g/1³/₄ oz plain wheat flour

100 g/3¹/₂ oz dark chocolate coating

300 g/10¹/₂ oz red wine cream (ready-made)

5 tbsp pear juice

125 g/4¹/₂ oz yoghurt

1 tbsp almond pieces

1. Mix the butter with the icing sugar, egg white and flour and stir together well. Preheat the oven to 200 °C/390 °F/gas mark 6.

2. Cover a baking tray with grease-proof paper. Roll the dough out onto a flour-covered working surface, and use a 10 cm/4 in template to cut into small circles. Place these on the baking tray and bake on the middle shelf of the oven for approx. 6 minutes.

3. Brush streaks of the chocolate coating onto the flat cakes. Prepare the red wine cream as instructed on the packaging.

4. Stir the pear juice and yoghurt together and then place in the fridge to set.

5. Finally fill into an icing bag and add swirls of cream to each cake. Serve garnished with the almonds.

Preparation time: approx. 30 minutes
Per serving: approx. 409 kcal/1718 kj,
5 g P, 10 g F, 72 g C

Quince cake

FOR 24 SERVINGS:

200 g/7 oz quark

8 tbsp oil

1 egg

200 g/7 oz sugar

600 g/1 lb 5 oz plain wheat flour

¹/₂ tsp baking powder

4 tbsp milk

1 kg/2 lbs 3 oz quinces

8 tbsp honey

2 tbsp lemon juice

A pinch of clove powder

100 ml/3¹/₂ fl oz dry sherry

100 g/3¹/₂ oz soft butter

Cinnamon powder

1. Drain the quark through a sieve, pressing lightly to rid excess liquid.

2. Mix in the oil, egg, 100 g/3¹/₂ oz of the sugar, 400 g/14 oz of the flour, the baking powder and milk and knead this all into a dough.

3. Cover a baking tray with greaseproof paper and smooth the dough onto it.

4. Wash and dry the quinces, then chop them in half and remove the cores. Slice into small wedges.

5. Add the wedges to a saucepan together with the honey, lemon juice, clove powder and sherry and bring briefly to the boil.

6. Spread the fruit onto the dough and leave to stand for approx. 10 minutes. Preheat the oven to 200 °C/390 °F/gas mark 6.

7. While waiting finely chop up the remaining sugar, flour, butter and cinnamon powder on a lightly floured working surface.

8. Sprinkle the crumbly cinnamon mix over the quince cake and bake on the middle shelf of the oven for approx. 45 minutes.

Preparation time: approx. 1 hour
(excluding standing time)
Per serving: approx. 233 kcal/939 kj,
4 g P, 8 g F, 8 g C

Step 2

Graham Pear Cake

FOR 24 SERVINGS:

300 g/10½ oz Graham
(coarse grained wheatmeal) flour

200 g/7 oz butter

70 g/2½ oz icing sugar

A pinch of salt

A pinch of grated rind
from an untreated lemon

1 egg

500 g/1 lb 2 oz pears

100 g/3½ oz quince jam

Icing sugar, to decorate

1. Mix the butter (cut into pieces) and add to the flour followed by the icing sugar, salt, lemon rind and egg. Finely chop this all up on a working surface and knead into dough.

2. Wash and peel the pears cut them in half, remove the cores and chop them into cubes. Together with the jam fold carefully into the dough. Roll into a ball, wrap in cling film and then leave to stand in a cool place for approx. one hour. Preheat the oven to 200 °C/ 390 °F/gas mark 6.

3. Cover a baking tray with greaseproof paper and spread the dough onto it. Place on the middle shelf of the oven and bake for approx. 40 minutes. Shortly before serving sprinkle with a little icing sugar.

Preparation time: approx. 50 minutes
(excluding standing time)
Per serving: approx. 144 kcal/608 kj,
2 g P, 7 g F, 16 g C

Step 2

Apple Cheese Cake

FOR 12 SERVINGS:

200 g/7 oz plain wheat flour

1 tsp baking powder

100 g/3$^{1}/_{2}$ oz butter

250 g/9 oz sugar

A pinch of salt

6 eggs

Lard, to grease the baking tin

700 g/1 lb 9 oz Mascarpone

2 cl/$^{1}/_{2}$ Calvados

300 g/10$^{1}/_{2}$ oz sour cream

3 tbsp cornflour

2 drops vanilla extract

1 tbsp lemon juice

1 tbsp rind of 1 untreated lemon

250 g/9 oz small apples

3 tbsp lemon juice

3 tbsp cake glaze

1. Mix the flour with the baking powder, butter, 75 g/2$^{1}/_{2}$ oz of the sugar, salt and one egg in a large bowl and then knead into a dough. Finally leave to stand in a cool place for approx. one hour.

2. Preheat the oven to 175 °C/ 350 °F/gas mark 3–4. Roll out the dough onto a flour-covered working surface. Grease a 28 cm/11 in springform baking tin with the lard and line it with the dough. Pre-bake on the middle shelf of the oven for approx. 15 minutes.

3. Stir the Mascarpone and Calvados together with the remaining sugar in a bowl. Separate the remaining eggs and whisk the egg yolks one by one into the cheese mix.

4. Fold in the sour cream. Stir the cornflour, vanilla extract, lemon juice, and lemon rind together and add. Whisk up the egg whites and fold into the mix.

5. Fill the pre-baked cake base with the finished mix and smooth the top off. Bake a further 60 minutes on the middle shelf of the oven. After approx. 30 minutes cover the top of the cake with aluminium foil or greaseproof paper to prevent it from becoming too brown.

6. Turn the oven off and allow the cake to stand in it for 15 minutes. Finally release the cake baking tin and remove the cheesecake.

7. Wash and peel the apples, cut them in half and remove the cores. Cut into wedges and sprinkle with the lemon juice, then arrange them on top of the cake, leaving a small gap near to the edges. Prepare the cake glaze according to the instructions on the packaging and then pour over the fruit.

Preparation time: approx. 50 minutes
(excluding standing time)
Per serving: approx.419 kcal/1763 kj,
13 g P, 22 g F, 36 g C

23

Sunken Pear Cake

FOR 12 SERVINGS:

200 g/7 oz dried plums

5 tbsp pear schnapps

400 g/14 oz firm pears

Butter, to grease the baking tin

Breadcrumbs for the baking tin

3 eggs

200 g/7 oz soft butter

200 g/7 oz sugar

1 tbsp vanilla sugar

250 g/9 oz plain wheat flour

A pinch of salt

2 tsp baking powder

25 g/1 oz chopped hazelnuts

1. Place the plums in a saucepan with a little water and bring to the boil briefly, then remove from heat and drain. Cut into very thin strips.

2. Sprinkle with the pear schnapps, cover and leave to draw for 20 minutes.

3. Wash and peel the pears, cut in half and remove the cores. Slice into wedges, add to boiling water and blanche for 1 minute. Remove from heat and immediately shock with cold water and drain.

4. Preheat the oven to 200 °C/ 390 °F/gas mark 6. Grease a 26 cm/10 in springform baking tin with butter, and sprinkle over the breadcrumbs. Separate the eggs.

5. Cream the butter together with the sugar, vanilla sugar and the egg yolk until light and fluffy.

6. Whisk the egg white until it is stiff. Mix the flour with the salt and baking powder. Fold the egg snow and the flour mix into the butter and sugar.

7. Turn the dough into the prepared baking tin and smooth off top. Add the plums as the first layer, pressing them in lightly (save some of the fruit to use as decoration at the end). Then put the pear slices on top. Decorate with the remaining plums and sprinkle everything with the hazelnuts.

8. Bake everything on the middle shelf of the oven for approx. 45 minutes.

Preparation time: approx. 50 minutes
Per serving: approx. 329 kcal/1384 kj,
4,5 g P, 17 g F, 36 g C

Apple Cinnamon Cake

FOR 12 SERVINGS:

100 g/3$^{1}/_{2}$ oz currants
100 g/3$^{1}/_{2}$ oz dried apple rings
5 tbsp white rum
200 g/7 oz butter
125 g/4$^{1}/_{2}$ oz sugar
1 tbsp vanilla sugar
2 eggs
A pinch of salt
1 tbsp cinnamon powder
125 g/4$^{1}/_{2}$ oz plain wheat flour
1 tsp baking powder
100 g/3$^{1}/_{2}$ oz ground walnuts
Butter, to grease baking tin
3 sugar coated apple slices, to garnish

1. Wash the currants and apple rings and add them to a bowl together with the rum. Leave to draw.

2. Cream the butter together with the sugar and vanilla sugar until it becomes light and fluffy. While doing this add the eggs one by one.

3. Continue to whisk until the sugar has completely dissolved. Stir the salt, cinnamon, flour, baking powder and the ground walnuts into the mixture. Carefully fold in the currants and the apple rings. Preheat the oven to 180 °C/ 355 °F/gas mark 4.

4. Take a 20 cm/8 in long loaf tin, grease the inside with butter and then add the dough to it. Smooth off the top, place it in the oven on the middle shelf and bake for approx. 50 minutes.

5. Tap the cake out of the tin, and then leave to cool down. Garnish with the sugar coated apple slices.

Preparation time: approx. 1 hour
Per serving: approx. 320 kcal/1347 kj,
4 g P, 19 g F, 29 g C

Step 2

Step 3

Sweet Brioche

FOR 8 SERVINGS:

160 ml/5¹/₂ fl oz milk

400 g/14 oz plain wheat flour

30 g/1 oz fresh yeast

60 g/2 oz butter

240 g/8¹/₂ oz sugar

A pinch of salt

1 egg

2 egg yolks

400 g/14 oz tinned pears

100 g/3¹/₂ oz raisins

Butter, to grease the casserole dish

2 cl pear liqueur

3 tbsp buckthorn jelly

100 g/3¹/₂ oz sugar

Decorating sugar

1. Warm the milk up in a saucepan. Sift the flour into a bowl and press down the middle to make a hollow, and then crumble the yeast into this. Pour the warm milk over it. Knead the mix together and leave in a warm place to rise for approx. 20 minutes.

2. Now add the butter, 40 g/¹/₂ oz of the sugar, salt, one egg and the egg yolk and again knead into a dough. Roll into a ball and then cover and leave until it has doubled in size.

3. Drain the pears and chop them into small cubes. Preheat the oven

to 160 °C/320 °F/gas mark 2–3. Grease a 20 cm/8 in casserole dish with some butter.

4. Gently fold in the pears, raisins, pear liqueur, buckthorn jelly and remaining sugar.

5. Roll the dough into a ball and place in the casserole leaving to rise a further 10 minutes. Place on the middle shelf of your oven and bake for approx. 60 minutes. Sprinkle with the decorating sugar and serve.

Preparation time: approx. 60 minutes
(excluding standing time)
Per serving: approx. 422 kcal/1772 kj,
9,5 g P, 11,5 g F, 64 g C

Tirol Apple Cake

FOR 24 SERVINGS:

300 g/10½ oz flaky pastry (frozen)

1 kg/2 lbs 3 oz cooking apples

Lemon juice

40 g/1½ oz sultanas

150 g/5 oz sugar

40 g/1½ oz chopped walnuts

A pinch of cinnamon powder

2 eggs

125 ml/4½ fl oz milk

Sugar and cinnamon, to decorate

1. Allow the flaky pastry to defrost according to the instructions on the packaging, and then roll flat on a flour-covered working surface to the size of the baking tray.

2. Preheat the oven to 220 °C/ 430 °F/gas mark 7. Cover the baking tray with greaseproof paper and place the dough on it.

3. Wash and peel the apples, cut in half and remove the cores, then cut again into quarters and finally into wedges. Sprinkle with some lemon juice. Coarsely chop the sultanas.

4. Mix together the apples, 100 g/ 3½ oz of the sugar, sultanas, almonds and cinnamon powder. Sprinkle over the dough.

5. Stir the eggs, milk and remaining sugar together and pour over the apples.

6. Bake everything on the middle shelf of the oven for approx. 40 minutes. Sprinkle with the sugar and cinnamon mix and serve.

Preparation time: approx. 50 min
Per serving: approx.127 kcal/533 kj,
1 g P, 5 g F, 15 g C

Colourful Pear Pie

FOR 12 SERVINGS:

300 g/10½ oz plain wheat flour
180 g/6½ oz butter
1 tbsp lard
Grated rind of ½ an untreated lemon
5 tbsp iced water
a pinch of salt
60 g/2 oz icing sugar
Flour, for rolling
Butter, to grease the baking tin
700 g/1 lb 9 oz pears
80 g/2¾ oz sugar
3 tbsp lemon juice
100 ml/3½ fl oz water
A pinch of cinnamon powder
200 g/7 oz blackberries
40 g/1½ oz amarettinis
1 egg yolk
Icing sugar, to decorate

1. Sift the flour onto a working surface and make a hollow into the middle. Distribute the butter and lard in small pieces around the edges of the flour.

2. Add the lemon rind, iced water, salt and 60 g/2 oz of the icing sugar to the hollow. Quickly knead the ingredients into smooth dough. Roll into a ball, wrap in cling film and leave to stand for approx. 1 hour in a cool place.

3. Preheat the oven to 220 °C/ 430 °F/gas mark 7. Roll the dough onto a flour-covered working surface and use it to line a 26 cm/ 10 in baking tin. Cut off the overlapping dough and roll together to make a lid. Peel the pears, cut them in half, remove the cores and cut into wedges. Mix 80 g/2¾ oz of the sugar with the lemon juice, cinnamon and 100 ml/3 ½ fl oz of the water into a saucepan and par boil. Wash and dry the blackberries.

4. Crush the amarettinis, mix with the fruit and pour onto the dough. Press the lid into place and cut a hole in the middle. Brush the pie once over with the egg yolk and bake on the middle shelf of the oven for 30 minutes. Sprinkle with the icing sugar and serve.

Preparation time: approx. 50 minutes
(excluding standing time)
Per serving: approx. 286 kcal/1201 kj,
3,5 g P, 15 g F, 30 g C

Caramel Tart

FOR 12 SERVINGS:

1 kg/2 lbs 3 oz apples
2 tbsp lemon juice
250 g/9 oz flaky pastry (frozen)
Flour, for rolling
Butter, to grease pie dish
3 tbsp breadcrumbs
180 g/6½ oz sugar
Lemon balm, to garnish

1. Wash and peel the apples, cut in half, remove the cores and cut into wedges, then sprinkle with

some lemon juice. Preheat the oven to 200 °C/390 °F/gas mark 6.

2. Roll the flaky pastry out flat on a flour-covered working surface and line a greased 30 cm/12 in pie dish with it.

3. Puncture the base of the dough several times with a fork and sprinkle over the breadcrumbs.

4. Pre-bake the base on the middle shelf of the oven for approx. 30 minutes.

5. Bring 125 ml/4¹/₂ fl oz water and 75 g/2¹/₂ oz sugar to the boil in a big flat saucepan, and until the sugar is completely dissolved.

6. Add the apple wedges and cook in the sugar syrup on a low heat for 1–2 minutes, turning continuously (the apple wedges should stay crunchy and keep their shape).

7. Drain and put the syrup to one side. Layer the fruit like roofing tiles on top of the flaky pastry. Stir the remaining sugar into the syrup. Heat the syrup up on high flame, until it turns a light brown colour.

8. Dribble the syrup over the apple wedges using a teaspoon.

Leave to cool and then serve garnished with lemon balm.

Preparation time: approx. 50 min
Per serving: approx. 211 kcal/886 kj,
1,5 g P, 7 g F, 32 g C

Step 3

Traditional German Apple Cake

FOR 12 SERVINGS:

750 g/1 lb 11 oz red apples

3 tbsp lemon juice

150 g/5 oz soft butter

200 g/7 oz sugar

A pinch of salt

1 tsp grated rind of 1 untreated lemon

3 eggs

200 g/7 oz plain wheat flour

1 tsp baking powder

200 g/7 oz rhubarb

Butter, to grease baking tin

3 tbsp apple jam

1. Wash and peel the apples, cut them in half and remove the cores. Slice into wedges and dribble some lemon juice over them.

2. Stir the butter, 150 g/5 oz of the sugar, the salt and lemon rind together into a creamy light consistency. Separate the eggs and fold the egg yolk into the mix.

3. Fold in the flour and baking powder. Wash the rhubarb, peeling if necessary and then slice into small pieces.

4. Add 50 g/1¾ oz of the sugar to the rhubarb and cook together in a saucepan for approx. 3 minutes until soft. Add the rhubarb mix to the dough. Whisk the egg white until it is stiff and then carefully fold into the dough.

5. Preheat the oven to 200 °C/ 390 F/gas mark 6. Take a 20 cm/ 8 in springform baking tin, grease with the butter and then add the dough to it.

6. Lay the apple slices on top. Heat the jam up in a saucepan and brush it onto the cake. Place in the oven on the middle shelf and bake for approx. 50 minutes.

Preparation time: approx. 1 hour
Per serving: approx. 273 kcal/1149 kj,
3,5 g P, 12 g F, 33 g C

Fruity Waffle Cake

FOR 24 SERVINGS:

400 g/14 oz waffle baking mixture

125 g/4½ oz soft butter

2 eggs

4 tbsp milk

Butter, to grease waffle iron

150 g/5 oz quince compote

4 tbsp rose hip purée

Icing sugar, to decorate

Grated chocolate, to garnish

1. Prepare the waffle dough according to the instructions on the packet and leave to stand.

2. Brush the waffle iron with some butter and warm it up.

3. Stir the quince compote together with the rose hip purée in a bowl.

4. Take small portions of the dough and bake each waffle on the iron. Spread the fruit mix over one waffle and place another on top to make a sandwich and then sprinkle with the icing sugar and garnish with the chocolate. Slice into triangular cake portions and serve.

Preparation time: approx. 40 minutes
Per serving: approx. 117 kcal/492 kj,
2 g P, 6 g F, 11 g C

Step 1

Summertime Cream Puffs

FOR 12 SERVINGS:

50 g/1³/₄ oz butter
A pinch of salt
150 g/5 oz plain wheat flour
4 eggs
2 apples
2 pears
200 g/7 oz blackberries
Lemon juice
1 tsp vanilla extract
1 tbsp vanilla sugar
250 ml/9 fl oz whipping cream
3 tbsp cream stabilizer (if needed)
Fruit, to garnish

1. Add the butter to 250 ml/9 fl oz water in a saucepan and bring to the boil. Preheat the oven to 200 °C/390 °F/gas mark 6.

2. Add the salt and flour to the butter and stir into a firm smooth dough. Place the dough mass into a bowl and one by one slowly knead the eggs in.

3. Cover a baking tray with grease-proof paper. Make small clumps of the dough using a tablespoon and put them on the paper, each about 5 cm/2 in apart. Place in the oven on the middle shelf and bake for approx. 20 minutes.

4. Wash and peel the apples and pears and cut them into small cubes. Wash and dry the black-berries. Add all the fruit to a saucepan and sprinkle with some lemon juice. Stir in the vanilla extract and vanilla sugar. Heat up gently and cook for approx. 4 minutes. Finally use a fork to press down the mixture into a purée and leave to cool.

5. Whisk the cream until it is stiff (add the cream stabilizer if need-ed) and then stir in the fruit mix. Remove the puffs, slice them in half and add the cream filling. Garnish with fruits of your choice and serve.

Preparation time: approx. 45 min
Per serving: approx. 146 kcal/614 kj,
2 g P, 9 g F, 11,5 g C

Crunchy Apple Cake

FOR 24 SERVINGS:

160 ml/5¹/₂ fl oz milk

400 g/14 oz plain wheat flour

30 g/1 oz fresh yeast

60 g/2 oz butter

40 g/1¹/₂ oz sugar

A pinch of salt

1 egg

1 egg yolk

1 kg/2 lbs 3 oz apples

150 g/5 oz cornflakes (crushed)

6 tbsp sugar-cinnamon mix

200 g/7 oz almond flakes (crushed)

100 g/3¹/₂ oz raisins

1. Warm the milk up in a saucepan. Sift the flour into a bowl, make a hollow in the middle of it and crumble the fresh yeast into it. Pour the milk onto the flour, knead everything together and leave to rise in a warm place for approx. 20 minutes.

2. Knead the butter, sugar, salt, egg and egg yolk into the dough. Roll into a ball, cover and leave again to rise to double its size.

3. While waiting wash and peel the apples, cutting them in half and removing the cores. Cut again into quarters and then slice into wedges. Preheat the oven to 200 °C/390 °F/gas mark 6.

4. Prepare a baking tray with greaseproof paper and roll the dough onto it. Sprinkle the corn-flakes over the dough together with half of the sugar-cinnamon mix.

5. Now distribute the apple wedges over the dough and sprinkle with the rest of the sugar-cinnamon mix, the almond flakes and raisins. Place in the oven on the middle shelf and bake for approx. 30 minutes.

Preparation time: approx. 45 minutes
Per serving: approx. 189 kcal/795 kj,
4 g P, 6 g F, 24 g C

Fine Fruit Ring Cake

FOR 12 SERVINGS:

400 g/14 oz marzipan cake mix

150 g/5 oz butter

250 g/9 oz apples

Lemon juice

3 eggs

150 g/5 oz ground almonds

Butter, to grease baking tin

2 tbsp breadcrumbs

150 ml/¼ pint cream

Icing sugar, to decorate

1. Take the marzipan from the cake mix and stir the butter into it. Wash and peel the apples and then grate them. Sprinkle with some lemon juice.

2. Preheat the oven to 220 °C/ 430 °F/gas mark 7. Fold the apple, cake mix, eggs and almonds into the marzipan mass.

3. Grease a ring cake baking tin with butter and sprinkle with the breadcrumbs. Fill the tin with the dough and smooth off the top. Place in the oven on the middle shelf and bake for 35 minutes.

4. Beat the cream to a firm consistency. Tap the cake out of the mould, garnish with the cream and sprinkle with the icing sugar and serve.

Preparation time: approx. 45 minutes
Per serving: approx. 335 kcal/1408 kj,
7 g P, 23 g F, 19 g C

Chocolate Grape Cake

FOR 12 SERVINGS:

400 g/14 oz chocolate cake mix (ready-made)

125 g/4½ oz butter

3 eggs

4 tbsp milk

30 g/1 oz desiccated coconut

Butter, to grease the baking tin

3 tbsp breadcrumbs

200 g/7 oz lemon cream (ready-made)

34

100 g/3¹/₂ oz Mascarpone

200 g/7 oz seedless green grapes

2 tbsp Grappa

Chocolate coating

Desiccated coconut, to garnish

1. Prepare the ready-made cake dough as described on the packaging. Grease a 20 cm/8 in long cake tin and sprinkle over the breadcrumbs. Preheat the oven to 180 °C/355 °F/gas mark 4.

2. Put the dough into the cake tin and place in the oven on the middle shelf and bake for approx. 50 minutes.

3. Prepare the lemon cream as instructed on the packaging. Stir in the Mascarpone. Wash the grapes and liquidise using a hand-blender. Add together with the Grappa to the cream mix. Leave to stand approx. 1 hour.

4. Remove the cake from the oven, leave to cool and then cut in half horizontally. Spread the lower half with the lemon-grape cream mix and sit the upper half on top. Brush the top with the chocolate coating, sprinkle with the coconut and serve.

Preparation time: approx. 1 hour (excluding cooling time)
Per serving: approx. 166 kcal/700 kj, 2,5 g P, 3 g F, 30 g C

Step 4

Sweet Soft
Stone Fruit Cakes

Apricots, plums, cherries, and more –
recipes for all tastes

Peach Cake

FOR 12 SERVINGS:

200 g/7 oz butter

3 eggs

1 stem of fresh vanilla

100 g/3½ oz sugar

200 g/7 oz plain wheat flour

A pinch of salt

1 tsp baking powder

Butter, to grease the baking tin

1 kg/2 lbs 3 oz peaches

50 g/1¾ oz honey

30 g/1 oz brown sugar

30 g/1 oz flaked almonds

1. Cream the butter until light and fluffy. Separate the eggs and add the egg yolk to the butter.

Squeeze the vanilla extract out of the middle of the stem and add to the butter together with the sugar. Preheat the oven to 200 °C/390 °F/ gas mark 6.

2. Sift the flour into the mix and add the baking powder and salt. Work everything into a smooth dough. If it becomes too hard, then simply add 2–3 tablespoons of milk.

3. Whisk the egg white into snow and fold carefully into the dough. Take a 26 cm/10 in springform baking tin and grease with butter. Line the tin with the dough and bake on the middle shelf of the oven for approx. 35 minutes.

4. Wash the peaches and score the skin with crosses, heat them well in a saucepan and then peel and half them. Remove the stones and cut into wedges.

5. Mix the honey, brown sugar and flaked almonds together and sprinkle over the peaches.

6. Now add the peach mix to the pre-baked dough and bake for a further 15 minutes. Remove from the oven when ready, release the springform and allow to cool.

Preparation time: approx. 1 hour
Per serving: approx.
315 kcal/1323 kj, 4,5 g P, 17 g F, 32 g C

Yellow Plum Cake

FOR 24 SERVINGS:

100 g/3¹/₂ oz soft butter

100 g/3¹/₂ oz sugar

1 tbsp vanilla sugar

A pinch of salt

100 g/3¹/₂ oz marzipan paste

3 eggs

150 g/5 oz plain wheat flour

50 g/1³/₄ oz cornflour

2 tsp baking powder

4 tbsp cream

750 g/1 lb 11 oz yellow plums (preserved)

300 g/10¹/₂ oz cherries (preserved)

4 tbsp lemon juice

6 cl Kirsch

60 g/2 oz breadcrumbs

2 tbsp honey

1. Mix together the butter, sugar, vanilla sugar, salt, crumbled marzipan and eggs thoroughly.

2. Add the flour, cornflour and baking powder while continuing to mix. Fold in the cream carefully. Preheat the oven to 200 °C/390 °F/ gas mark 6.

3. Drain the plums and cherries thoroughly. Mix in the lemon juice and Kirsch, cover and leave to marinate for approx. 10 minutes.

4. Roll out the dough and spread onto a baking tray covered with greaseproof paper. Score the surface with a fork and sprinkle with the breadcrumbs. Drain the marinade from the fruit and keep. Spread the fruit over the dough, place on the middle shelf of the oven and bake for approx. 35 minutes.

5. Heat the marinade together with the honey in a saucepan until the mix is thick and runny. Shortly before the baking time is complete brush onto the cake and continue to bake until caramelised (approx. 5 minutes).

Preparation time: approx. 50 minutes
Per serving: approx. 148 kcal/625 kj,
2,5 g P, 5,5 g F, 20 g C

Fruity Cheese Cake

FOR 24 SERVINGS:

300 g/10$\frac{1}{2}$ oz quark

8 tbsp oil

5 eggs

300 g/10$\frac{1}{2}$ oz sugar

575 g/1 lb 4 oz plain wheat flour

$\frac{1}{2}$ tsp baking powder

4 tbsp milk

750 g/1 lb 11 oz cream cheese

1 tsp grated rind of lemon

1 tbsp lemon juice

3 heaped tbsp custard powder

1 tbsp starch

200 g/7 oz butter

1 kg/2 lbs 3 oz apricot halves (tinned)

1 tbsp vanilla sugar

1. Drain the quark in a sieve, pressing out the excess liquid.

2. Mix the quark with the oil, 3 eggs, 100 g/3$\frac{1}{2}$ oz of the sugar, 400 g/14 oz of the flour, baking powder and milk and knead into a smooth dough.

3. Roll the dough out on a grease-proof paper covered baking tray. Preheat the oven to 180 °C/355 °F/ gas mark 4.

4. Separate the rest of the eggs. Stir together the cream cheese, lemon rind and lemon juice in one bowl. In another stir together the custard powder, starch, 100 g/ 3$\frac{1}{2}$ oz sugar, 100 g/3$\frac{1}{2}$ oz butter with the egg yolk. Whisk the egg white into snow and carefully add 50 g/1$\frac{3}{4}$ oz of sugar to it. Add all of this to the cheese mix by gently folding it in. Brush the resulting mix onto the dough.

5. Drain the apricots and lay them with the inside half facing down on the cream. Mix the vanilla sugar with the remaining flour and sugar. Melt the remaining butter and add. Chop the mix with a knife to make a crumble.

6. Cover the apricots and cream with the crumble, place on the middle shelf of the oven and bake for approx. 40 minutes.

Preparation time: approx. 1 hour
Per serving: approx. 311 kcal/1308 kj,
9 g P, 17 g F, 95 g C

Rhineland Cherry Slice

FOR 24 SERVINGS:

160 ml/5¹/₂ fl oz milk

400 g/14 oz plain wheat flour

30 g/1 oz fresh yeast

60 g/2 oz butter

40 g/1¹/₂ oz sugar

A pinch of salt

6 eggs

1 egg yolk

1 kg/2 lbs 3 oz sour cherries

Butter, to grease the tray

2 tsp cinnamon powder

400 g/14 oz double cream

6 tbsp vanilla sugar

1. Heat the milk in a saucepan. Sift the flour into a bowl, and make a hollow in the middle.

Crumble the yeast into the hollow. Pour the milk over this. Knead everything together, and leave to rise in a warm place for approx. 20 minutes.

2. Add the butter, sugar, salt, 1 egg and the egg yolk and knead together. Roll into a ball and cover, leaving again to rise and double in size.

3. Drain the sour cherries. Preheat the oven to 200 °C/390 °F/gas mark 6.

4. Roll the dough onto a flour-covered work surface. Place the dough onto a greased baking tray and cover with the sour cherries. Stir together the remaining eggs

with the cinnamon, double cream and vanilla sugar. Pour it over the cherries. Place on the middle shelf of the oven and bake for approx. 40 minutes.

Preparation time: approx. 50 minutes
(excluding standing time)
Per serving: approx. 186 kcal/781 kj,
5 g P, 9 g F, 17 g C

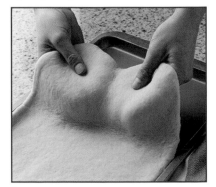

Step 5

Fruit Ice Cream Cake

FOR 12 SERVINGS:

600 g/1 lb 5 oz ripe apricots

80 g/2³/₄ oz sugar

4 cl/scant tsp apricot liqueur

1 l/1³/₄ pints vanilla ice cream

250 g/9 oz figs

250 ml/9 fl oz cream

1 tbsp vanilla sugar

200 g/7 oz butter biscuits

2 tbsp chopped pistachios

1. Wash and dry the apricots, score crosses into the skin, scald and peel them, removing the stones. Liquidise the remaining flesh using a hand-blender.

2. Stir the sugar and apricot liqueur into the purée, cover and leave to draw for 5 minutes.

3. Allow the vanilla ice cream to defrost a little. Wash and peel the figs and then cut them into wedges.

4. Beat the cream together with the vanilla sugar until stiff and fluffy. Add half of this to an icing bag and place in the fridge to cool for approx. 5 minutes.

5. Take a 20 cm/8 in bread tin and line it with aluminium foil and place a layer of the butter biscuits on the base. Mix the fruit purée together with the ice cream and spoon half of it onto the biscuits. Cover this with another layer of biscuits and put the figs on top and spread with some cream. Again cover this with a layer of biscuits. Spoon the remaining ice cream mix on top and cover with the remaining figs. Freeze the resulting cake and decorate with the remaining cream and pistachios before serving.

Preparation time: approx. 1 hour
Per serving: approx. 224 kcal/943 kj,
3 g P, 9 g F, 30 g C

42

Nectarine Quark Pastries

FOR 6 SERVINGS:

200 g/7 oz flaky pastry (frozen)

350 g/12 oz nectarines

Juice and rind of ½ an untreated lemon

100 g/3½ oz low fat quark

2 egg yolks

1 tbsp vanilla sugar

1 tbsp sugar

1 tbsp milk

Icing sugar, to decorate

1. Roll out the pastry and cut into six portions on a flour-covered working surface.

2. Wash the nectarines, score the skin and scald until soft, then peel and cut in half, removing the stones. Cut them into wedges and sprinkle with some lemon juice. Preheat the oven to 200 °C/390 °F/ gas mark 6.

3. Mix the quark together with one egg yolk, vanilla sugar, sugar, lemon rind and the remaining lemon juice.

4. Spread some of the quark mix onto the middle of each portion of

pastry. Fold the corners inwards and place some nectarine wedges on each.

5. Mix the milk with the remaining egg yolk and brush this onto the pastries.

6. Place all of them onto a grease-proof paper covered baking tray. Place on the middle shelf of the oven and bake for approx. 25 minutes. Decorate with icing sugar and then serve.

Preparation time: approx. 50 minutes
Per serving: approx. 234 kcal/986 kj,
3 g P, 14 g F, 20 g C

Sweet Cherry Tartlets

FOR 10 SERVINGS:

150 g/5 oz almond biscuits
60 g/2 oz butter
1 tbsp cherry jam
10 paper cake cups
350 g/12 oz cherries
1 cl/$^1/_4$ tsp Grappa
6 small sprigs of fresh mint
1 egg
150 g/5 oz ricotta
2 leaves white gelatine

1. Crumble the almond biscuits. Melt the butter and mix with the biscuits crumbs and cherry jam.

2. Scoop 2 tablespoons of the biscuit mix into each paper cake cup and press down to cover the base. Leave in a cool place for approx. 15 minutes.

3. Wash and dry the cherries, placing some to the side for decorating. Cut the rest in half and remove the stones, placing them in a bowl with the Grappa. Wash and dry the mint sprigs and add to the cherries, again leaving a few to garnish with later. Liquidise everything with a hand-blender and leave to draw for 15 minutes.

4. Separate the egg, and beat the egg white into snow. Stir the egg yolk together with the ricotta and cherry purée. Carefully fold the egg snow in the mix.

5. Soak the gelatine leaves in cold water, press excess liquid out and heat gently to dissolve. Carefully stir into the cherry-cheese cream mix and then add to an icing bag with a star-shaped nozzle. Fill each paper cake cup with the cream mix and decorate with the left over cherries and mint.

Preparation time: approx. 1 hour
Per serving: approx. 232kcal/976 kj,
7 g P, 18 g F, 6 g C

Plum Tart

FOR 12 SERVINGS:

150 g/5 oz flaky pastry (frozen)
500 g/1 lb 2 oz Victoria plums
80 g/2$^3/_4$ oz sugar
4 tbsp lemon juice
200 g/7 oz sponge fingers
8 tbsp sweet sherry
100 g/3$^1/_2$ oz ground hazelnuts
Butter, to grease the pie dish
Sugar, to decorate

1. Roll the flaky pastry out onto a flour-covered working surface. Take a 20 cm/8 in pie dish, turn over and lay flat on the pastry. Cut out a lining for the dish.

2. Slice the remaining pastry into strips. Wash the plums and cut in half removing the stones. Mix in the sugar and lemon juice.

3. Crumble the sponge fingers into the plums. Fold in the sherry and ground hazelnuts. Preheat the oven to 220 °C/430 °F/gas mark 7.

4. Brush the inside of the pie dish with melted butter and lay the pastry lining inside it. Spread the plum mixture on top. Brush cold water along the edge of the top pastry. Decorate across the top of the filling with the pastry strips.

5. Brush cold water over the top of the tart and sprinkle with sugar. Place on the middle shelf of your oven and bake for 30 minutes.

Preparation time: approx. 45 minutes
Per serving: approx. 182 kcal/767 kj,
2 g P, 9 g F, 19 g C

Step 4

Cherry Cake with a Kick

FOR 12 SERVINGS:

250 g/9 oz plain wheat flour

3 eggs

A pinch of salt

220 g/8 oz sugar

1 tbsp vanilla sugar

125 g/4¹/₂ oz butter

Butter, to grease baking tin

Breadcrumbs

600 g/1 lb 5 oz sour cherries

60 g/2 oz macaroons

80 g/2³/₄ oz icing sugar

6 tbsp cherry liqueur

125 ml/4¹/₂ fl oz whipping cream

40 g/1¹/₂ oz flaked hazelnuts

1. Sift the flour onto a working surface, and make a hollow in the middle of it. Add an egg and salt. Sprinkle with 100 g/3¹/₂ oz of the sugar and vanilla sugar. Distribute the butter in pieces around the edge of the flour. Chop all the ingredients together and then knead it all together into a smooth dough.

2. Roll the dough into a large ball, wrap in cling film and leave to stand for approx. 1 hour. Take a 26 cm/10 in springform baking tin and grease the inside with butter and then sprinkle with breadcrumbs. Preheat the oven to 180 °C/355 °F/gas mark 4.

3. Line the baking tin with the dough, including a sidewall. Take a fork and puncture the pastry several times. Place on the middle shelf of the oven and bake for approx. 20 minutes.

4. Drain the sour cherries, add 100 g/3¹/2 oz of the sugar to them and allow to draw. Crumble the macaroons and sprinkle over the cake base. Spread the cherries on top of this.

5. Beat together the egg yolk of 2 eggs, the icing sugar and the cherry liqueur until light and fluffy. Whisk the remaining 2 egg whites and cream separately until stiff. Fold the two mixtures carefully together and spoon over the cherries. Place on the middle shelf of the oven and bake for approx. 30 minutes.

6. After 5 minutes baking time sprinkle the hazelnut flakes and remaining sugar over the top. Bake for the remaining time, remove and allow to cool on a cake rack before serving.

Preparation time: approx. 50 minutes
Per serving: approx. 314 kcal/1318 kj,
5 g P, 15 g F, 35 g C

Damson Cake on a Tray

FOR 12 SERVINGS:

420 g/14¾ oz plain wheat flour

20 g/¾ oz fresh yeast

50 g/1¾ oz sugar

125 ml/4½ fl oz milk

1.5 kg/3 lb 5 oz damsons

3 tbsp lemon juice

A pinch of salt

80 g/2¾ oz butter

2 eggs

400 ml/14 fl oz whipping cream

50 g/1¾ oz honey

30 g/1 oz brown sugar

200 g/7 oz almond flakes

1. Sift 350 g/12 oz of the flour onto a working surface and make a hollow in the middle. Gently heat up the milk and add a little sugar and crumble the yeast into it. Pour into the hollow and slowly mix the flour in, making the mix into a dough. Leave to stand and rise in warm place for approx. 20 minutes.

2. Wash and dry the damsons, cut in half, remove the stones and sprinkle with some lemon juice. Preheat the oven to 180 °C/355 °F/ gas mark 4.

3. Knead the dough with the rest of the flour, sugar, salt, eggs and butter. Cover and allow to rise a further 30 minutes. Mix together the cream, honey and brown sugar and bring to the boil, cooking for approx. 5 minutes. Stir an little flour in quickly. Fold in the almond flakes.

4. Roll the dough out and place on a baking tray covered with greaseproof paper, making a pronounced edge. Puncture the dough with a fork several times. Cover the dough completely with the damson mix and brush over with the almond mix. Place the cake on the middle shelf of the oven and bake for approx. 35 minutes. If necessary cover the top with greaseproof paper to prevent burning.

Preparation time: approx. 50 minutes
Per serving: approx. 419 kcal/1761 kj,
8,5 g P, 21 g F, 42 g C

Cherry Cake with Crème Fraîche

FOR 12 SERVINGS:

100 g/3¹/₂ oz plain wheat flour
2 tbsp ground almonds
60 g/2 oz cold butter, chopped
1 tbsp icing sugar
A pinch of salt
2 egg yolks
Butter, to grease baking tin
400 g/14 oz cherries
250 g/9 oz crème fraîche
2 tbsp icing sugar
1 tbsp vanilla sugar
¹/₂ tsp rind of 1 untreated lemon
Cocoa powder, to decorate

1. Mix the flour with 1 tablespoon of the ground almonds, butter pieces, icing sugar, salt and an egg yolk and knead all together into a smooth dough. Wrap in cling film and leave in the fridge to cool for 30 minutes.

2. Preheat the oven to 180 °C/ 355 °F/gas mark 4 and grease an 18 cm/7 in springform baking tin with butter.

3. Wash and dry the cherries and remove the stones. Roll the dough between some cling film to the size of the baking tin's base and line the springform with it, making sure to make a small edging.

4. Puncture the dough several times with a fork and sprinkle over with the remaining ground almonds.

5. Stir the crème fraîche with the remaining egg yolk, icing sugar, vanilla sugar and lemon rind into smooth paste.

6. Brush some of this paste onto the base. Pour the cherries into the springform and cover with the remaining cream paste.

7. Place on the middle shelf of the oven and bake for approx. 40 minutes.

8. Open the springform and remove the cake, allow to cool and then sprinkle with the cocoa powder.

Preparation time: approx. 1 hour
(excluding standing time)
Per serving: approx. 187 kcal/788 kj,
2,5 g P, 13,5 g F, 10 g C

Peach and Cranberry Cake

FOR 24 SERVINGS:

160 ml/5¹/₂ fl oz milk

400 g/14 oz plain wheat flour

30 g/1 oz fresh yeast

60 g/2 oz butter

40 g/1¹/₂ oz sugar

A pinch of salt

1 egg

1 egg yolk

800 g/1 lb 12 oz peach halves (tinned)

500 g/1 lb 2 oz cranberry jam

3 tbsp lemon juice

4 cl/scant tsp pear schnapps

300 g/10¹/₂ oz white cake glaze

3 tbsp coconut oil

1. Heat the milk in a saucepan. Sift the flour into a bowl and make a hollow in it. Crumble the yeast into the hollow. Pour the milk over this. Knead briefly into a dough and leave in a warm place to rise for 20 minutes.

2. Carefully knead in the butter, sugar, salt, egg and egg yolk and make into a smooth dough. Roll into a ball, cover a allow to rise until it is twice it's original size.

3. Preheat the oven to 200 °C/ 390 °F/gas mark 6. Drain the peaches.

4. Roll out the dough and place on a baking tray covered in grease-proof paper. Spread with the cranberry jam and add the peaches pressing them into the dough. Leave to rise a further 10 minutes.

5. Place on the middle shelf of the oven and bake for approx. 30 minutes.

6. Fill a plastic bag with the pear schnapps, coating and coconut oil. Heat up over a saucepan of water and carefully knead together. Cut one of the corners of the bag off and immediately run over the cake decorating it with stripes.

Preparation time: approx. 45 min
Per serving: approx. 226 kcal/949 kj,
4 g P, 4 g F, 40 g C

Step 4

Plum Strudel

FOR 6 SERVINGS:

200 g/7 oz plain wheat flour
3 tbsp oil
A pinch of salt
750 g/1 lb 11 oz plums
Juice and rind of ¹/₂ an untreated lemon
5 tbsp sugar
¹/₂ tsp cinnamon powder
60 g/2 oz butter
5 tbsp grated almonds
Icing sugar, to decorate

1. Mix the flour with the oil, salt and 150 ml/1/4 pint water in a bowl and knead together. Roll into a ball, wrap in cling film and place in a fridge to cool for 30 minutes.

2. Wash and dry the plums, cut in half and remove the stones. Place in a bowl and mix in the lemon juice, lemon rind, 5 tablespoons of the sugar and cinnamon. Leave to draw for approx. 30 minutes.

3. Preheat the oven to 200 °C/390 °F/gas mark 6. Roll the dough out thinly on a flour-covered working surface. Pull over the back of your hand into a 50 cm/20 in square.

4. Lay on a flour-covered clean kitchen towel. Melt the butter and brush it onto the dough.

5. Sprinkle the dough with the almonds and plums. Lift the edge of the kitchen towel and roll the dough together. Place on a baking tray covered with greaseproof paper. Place on the middle shelf of the oven and bake for approx. 35 minutes. When ready sprinkle with icing sugar and cut into slices.

Preparation time: approx. 45 min
Per serving: approx. 187 kcal/788 kj,
2,5 g P, 13,5 g F, 10 g C

Little Peach Cakes

FOR 4 SERVINGS:

75 g/2½ oz butter

75 g/2½ oz sugar

1 egg

A pinch of salt

20 g/¾ oz cornflour

3 tbsp milk

125 g/4½ oz plain wheat flour

1 tbsp baking powder

100 ml/3½ fl oz chocolate sauce (ready-made)

12 peach halves (tinned)

Lemon balm, to garnish

1. Mix the butter with the sugar, egg and salt in a bowl. Stir the cornflour, milk, flour and baking powder into the butter mix. Fold in 3 tablespoons of the chocolate sauce. Preheat the oven to 180 °C/ 355 °F/gas mark 4.

2. Split the dough into 4 portions and place it on a baking tray covered with greaseproof paper.

3. Use a spoon to smooth out the dough into circular bases (approx. 8 cm/3¼ in). Drain the peach halves. Cut the peach halves into wedges and arrange in star formations on the pastry bases and press into the dough.

4. Use a spoon to smooth out the dough into circular bases (8 cm/ 3¼ in). Drain the peach halves.

5. Bake for approx. 15 minutes on the middle shelf of the oven.

6. Place the small cakes on a plate and garnish with the lemon balm. Decorate them with the remaining chocolate sauce.

Preparation time: approx. 30 minutes
Per serving: approx. 503 kcal/2114 kj,
7 g P, 22 g F, 64 g C

Step 3

Traditional English Fruit Pie

FOR 12 SERVINGS:

375 g/13 oz plain wheat flour

75 g/2½ oz butter

150 g/5 oz margarine

70 g/2½ oz sugar

Salt

450 g/1 lb yellow plums

3 nectarines

120 g/5 oz sugar

Rind of 1 untreated lemon

1 tbsp cornflour

1 egg

1. Mix the flour with the butter, margarine, 70 g/2½ oz sugar, salt and 100 ml/3½ fl oz ice cold water and knead the mixture into a smooth dough. Roll into a ball, wrap in cling film and leave to stand for 1 hour in a cold place.

2. Split the dough in half and roll one half into a circle 32 cm/12¾ in diameter (or at least 8 cm/3¼ in larger than the dish). To centre the dough fold into quarters and place the middle point in the middle of a 24 cm/9½ in pie dish and unfold.

3. Wash the plums, cut them in half and remove the stones. Wash the nectarines, cut in half and remove the stones and cut into wedges. Preheat the oven to 180 °C/355 °F/gas mark 4.

4. Take half of the fruit and heat up in a saucepan together with 120 g/5 oz sugar, lemon rind and cornflour. Fold in the rest of the fruit. Distribute the fruit mix over the dough.

5. Roll the other half of the dough into a 30 cm/12 in round lid and lay over the pie filling. Press the overlapping edges together to the lid edges and use your fingers to press decorative waves along the rim.

6. Beat the egg and brush the dough with it. Place on the middle shelf of the oven and bake for approx. 50 minutes.

Preparation time: approx. 1 hour
Per serving: approx. 305 kcal/1281 kj,
4 g P, 15 g F, 33 g C

Apricot Slices

FOR 12 SERVINGS:

8 eggs

200 g/7 oz sugar

A pinch of salt

100 g/3½ oz plain wheat flour

100 g/3½ oz ground hazelnuts

A pinch of baking powder

A pinch of cinnamon powder

6 leaves of white gelatine

Juice and rind of 2 untreated lemons

¼ l/9 fl oz dry white wine

4 cl/scant tsp Armagnac (brandy)

125 ml/4½ fl oz whipping cream

500 g/1 lb 2 oz apricots

1. Separate the eggs. Beat 5 egg yolks with 4 tablespoon of cold water until light and fluffy, while drizzling in 100 g/3½ oz of the sugar. Preheat the oven to 200 °C/ 390 °F/gas mark 6.

2. In a second bowl beat 4 egg whites with a pinch of salt into snow and add 50 g/1¾ oz sugar at the end.

3. Slide the snow onto the egg yolk mix. Mix the flour with the ground hazelnuts, baking and cinnamon powder and fold this carefully into the egg mix. Prepare a baking tray with greaseproof paper and slowly spread the dough onto it.

4. Place on the middle shelf of the oven and bake for approx. 15 minutes. When ready drop onto a cake rack and remove the paper and allow to cool.

5. Cut the cake into equal 10 cm/ 4 in slices.

6. Soak the gelatine in cold water. Beat the rest of the egg yolk with the remaining sugar, lemon juice, lemon rind, white wine and Armagnac in a bowl until foamy. Place the bowl in a hot water jacket and continue beating until the mixture gets thicker. Press the gelatine out, allow to dissolve, while stirring in some of the cream mix. Complete by adding the rest of the mix.

7. Place in the fridge to cool and gel. Separately beat the remaining egg white with the whipping cream until stiff. Shortly before the cream mix in the fridge has completely gelled carefully fold in the whipping cream.

8. Cut the cake slices in half and spread most of the cream on the

lower half. Wash and dry the apricots, cut into wedges and use most of them to place on the cream layer. Place the top cake half on the fruit and decorate with the remaining cream and apricots.

Preparation time: approx. 1 hour
Per serving: approx. 281 kcal/1181 kj,
7 g P, 12 g F, 28 g C

Step 3

53

Spicy Fruit Tart

FOR 12 SERVINGS:

200 g/7 oz plain wheat flour

100 g/3½ oz sugar

100 g/3½ oz butter

3 eggs

1 egg yolk

A pinch of salt

Lard, to grease the pie dish

250 g/9 oz pumpkin pulp (in a jar)

400 g/14 oz nectarines

100 g/3½ oz brown sugar

100 g/3½ oz sour cream

2 tbsp chopped cashew nuts

A pinch of cinnamon powder

A pinch of clove powder

1 tbsp cornflour

Walnut kernels, to garnish

Icing sugar, to decorate

1. Mix together the flour with the sugar, butter, one egg, the egg yolk and salt in a bowl and knead it all together. Leave the dough to stand in a cool place for 1 hour.

2. Take a 26 cm/10 in pie dish or flan tin. Drain the pumpkin pulp. Scald the nectarines, peel and chop into small pieces. Liquidise the both using a hand-blender.

3. Preheat the oven to 200 °C/390 °F/gas mark 6. Roll the dough out on a working surface and line the pie dish with it making sure that the edge is at least 3 cm/1¼ in thick.

4. Separate the remaining eggs. Beat the egg whites into a stiff snow. Mix the egg yolk with the brown sugar, sour cream, cashew nuts and the spices and stir it all

together. Fold into the pumpkin purée while gradually adding the cornflour and egg snow. Spoon everything into the pie dish and place on the middle shelf of the oven and bake for approx. 50 minutes. Garnish with the walnuts and sprinkle with the icing sugar.

Preparation time: approx. 1 hour
Per serving: approx. 260 kcal/1092 kj,
4,5 g P, 11 g F, 33 g C

Step 2

54

Cherry Quark Cake

FOR 24 SERVINGS:

160 ml/5½ fl oz milk
400 g/14 oz plain wheat flour
30 g/1 oz fresh yeast
60 g/2 oz butter
240 g/8½ oz sugar
A pinch of salt
1 egg
3 egg yolks
800 g/1 lb 12 oz sour cherries (in a jar)
500 g/1 lb 2 oz low fat quark
40 g/1½ oz ground almonds
30 g/1 oz starch
1 tbsp rum
125 ml/4½ fl oz whipping cream
Icing sugar, to decorate

1. Heat the milk in a saucepan. Sift the flour into a bowl, make a hollow in the middle and crumble the yeast into it. Pour the milk over it. Knead everything together and leave to rise in a warm place for approx. 20 minutes.

2. Knead the butter, 40 g/1½ oz of the sugar, salt, one egg and 2 egg yolks into the dough. Roll everything into a ball and cover leaving to rise further until the dough has doubled its volume.

3. Drain the sour cherries. Preheat the oven to 200 °C/390 °F/gas mark 6. Cover a baking tray with greaseproof paper and roll the dough onto it.

4. Spread the cherries onto the dough. Drain the quark and beat together with the remaining sugar and egg yolk until foamy. Fold in the almonds, starch and rum. Whip the cream until stiff and fork into the quark mix.

5. Spread the cream onto the cherries and place in the oven on the middle shelf of the oven and bake for approx. 30 minutes. Dust with icing sugar before serving.

Preparation time: approx. 45 minutes (excluding standing time)
Per serving: approx. 166 kcal/700 kj, 6 g P, 7 g F, 18 g C

Traditional German Mirabella Cake

FOR 24 SERVINGS:

160 ml/5½ fl oz milk
400 g/14 oz plain wheat flour
30 g/1 oz fresh yeast
60 g/2 oz butter
40 g/1½ oz sugar
A pinch of salt
1 egg
1 egg yolk
1 kg/2 lbs 3 oz yellow plums
100 g/3½ oz chopped walnuts
100 g/3½ oz brown sugar

1. Heat the milk in a saucepan. Sift the flour into a bowl, make a hollow in the middle and crumble the yeast into it. Pour the milk over it. Knead everything together and leave to rise in a warm place for approx. 20 minutes.

2. Knead the butter, sugar, salt, egg and egg yolk into the dough. Roll everything into a ball and cover leaving to rise further until the dough has doubled its volume.

3. Preheat the oven to 200 °C/ 390 °F/gas mark 6. Wash the plums and cut in half removing the stones.

4. Cover a baking tray with greaseproof paper and roll the dough onto it.

5. Spread the plums over the dough and sprinkle with the walnuts and brown sugar. Place on the middle shelf of the oven and bake for approx. 30 minutes.

Preparation time: approx. 45 minutes
Per serving: approx. 163 kcal/685 kj,
4 g P, 5 g F, 22 g C

Plum Layer Cake

FOR 12 SERVINGS:

250 g/9 oz flaky pastry (frozen)
150 g/5 oz white cake glaze
250 ml/9 fl oz whipping cream
500 g/1 lb 2 oz plums
50 g/1³/₄ oz sugar
2 tbsp lemon juice
2 cl/¹/₂ tsp plum schnapps
Icing sugar, to decorate

1. Preheat the oven to 220 °C/ 430 °F/gas mark 7. Roll the sheets of flaky pastry into a flour-covered working surface and make 3 round plates of dough, using the 26 cm/ 10 in springform base as a template.

2. Prepare 2 baking trays with greaseproof paper, and place the sheets of dough on them. Place on the middle shelf of the oven and bake for approx. 20 minutes.

3. Mix the cake glaze with the cream, add to a saucepan and melt together on a gentle heat.

4. Allow to cool and leave to stand in a cool place. Wash and dry the plums, cut in half and remove the stones. Add to a saucepan together with the sugar, lemon juice and the plum schnapps and bring to the boil.

5. Whip the chocolate cream until it is stiff. Arrange half of the plums on the lower pastry layer and cover with half of the cream.

6. Place the next pastry layer on top and add the rest of the plums on top of this. Spread the rest of the cream onto the plums. Place the last pastry layer on top, press down lightly and decorate with icing sugar before serving.

Preparation time: approx. 45 minutes
Per serving: approx. 247 kcal/1038 kj,
2,5 g P, 13 g F, 26 g C

Step 1

Step 5

57

Topped Apricot Cake

For 24 servings:

150 g/5 oz buckwheat flour

150 g/5 oz maize flour

200 g/7 oz butter, chopped

170 g/5¹/₂ oz icing sugar

A pinch of salt

A pinch of grated rind of 1 untreated lemon

1 egg

1 kg/2 lbs 3 oz apricots (tinned)

200 g/7 oz apricot jam

3 egg whites

50 g/1³/₄ oz ground almonds

1. Add the flour, butter, 70 g/2¹/₂ oz of the icing sugar, salt, lemon rind and the egg to a working surface and chop up finely. Then knead this all together and roll into a ball. Wrap in cling film and leave in a cool place for 1 hour. Preheat the oven to 200 °C/390 °F/gas mark 6.

2. Drain the apricots. Cover a baking tray with greaseproof paper and roll the dough onto it. Spread the jam onto the dough and distribute the apricots on top. Place on the middle shelf of the oven and bake for approx. 30 minutes.

3. Beat the egg white until stiff and sprinkle over with the icing sugar and almonds.

4. 10 minutes before the completed baking time brush the egg meringue topping on to the apricots and return to the middle shelf to continue baking.

Preparation time: approx. 50 minutes
Per serving: approx. 169 kcal/713 kj,
2 g P, 8 g F, 18 g C

Preparation time: approx. 50 minutes
Per serving: approx. 170 kcal/714 kj,
3 g P, 5 g F, 23 g C

Nectarine Cake

FOR 24 SERVINGS:

160 ml/5¹/₂ fl oz milk

500 g/1 lb 2 oz plain wheat flour

30 g/1 oz fresh yeast

110 g/4 oz butter

40 g/1¹/₂ oz sugar

A pinch of salt

1 egg

1 egg yolk

20 g/³/₄ oz icing sugar

1 tbsp cinnamon powder

1 kg/2 lbs 3 oz nectarine

25 ground hazelnuts

80 g/2³/₄ oz quince jam

1. Heat the milk in a saucepan. Sift 400 g/14 oz of the flour into a bowl, and make a hollow in the middle. Pour the milk over it. Knead everything together and leave to rise in a warm place for approx. 20 minutes.

2. Mix 60 g/2 oz of the butter with the sugar, salt, egg and egg yolk and knead it all together. Finally roll everything into a ball and cover leaving to rise further until the dough has doubled its volume.

3. Finely chop the remaining flour with the remaining butter, icing sugar and cinnamon powder to make a crumble mixture. Preheat the oven to 200 °C/390 °F/gas mark 6.

4. Wash the nectarines, score with a knife and scald them. Peel, cut in half and remove the stones, cut again into quarters and then into wedges.

5. Cover a baking tray with greaseproof paper and roll the dough onto it, then sprinkle with the hazelnuts.

6. Spread the nectarine wedges on the dough and sprinkle with the crumble.

7. Place on the middle shelf of the oven and bake for approx. 30 minutes. Heat the jam in a saucepan and spread over the cake before serving.

Vanilla Pear Cake

FOR 24 SERVINGS:

460 ml/16 fl oz milk
400 g/14 oz flour
30 g/1 oz fresh yeast
210 g/7½ oz butter
80 g/2¾ oz sugar
A pinch of salt
5 eggs
1 egg yolk
300 g/10½ oz pears (tinned)
1 packet (3 heaped tbsp) vanilla pudding powder
300 g/10½ oz cream quark
2 cl/½ tsp pear liqueur
1 stem of vanilla
Icing sugar, to decorate

1. Heat 160 ml/5½ fl oz of the milk in a saucepan. Sift the flour into a bowl, make a hollow in the middle and crumble the yeast into it. Pour the milk over it. Knead everything together and leave to rise in a warm place for approx. 20 minutes.

2. Knead in 60 g/2 oz of the butter, 40 g/1½ oz of the sugar, salt, 1 egg and the egg yolk. Roll everything into a ball and cover leaving to rise further until the dough has doubled its volume.

3. Preheat the oven to 200 °C/390 °F/gas mark 6. Drain the pears and cut into wedges. Mix the remaining milk and 2 tablespoons sugar with the vanilla pudding and prepare as described on the packaging. Stir in the rest of the butter.

4. Separate the rest of the eggs. Mix the quark in a bowl with the pear liqueur, pears and vanilla paste (squeeze out of stem). Beat the egg white until stiff and fold in carefully. Roll the dough out and place onto a greaseproof paper covered baking tray.

5. Spread the mix onto the dough and Place on the middle shelf of the oven and bake for approx. 20 minutes. Sprinkle with icing sugar before serving.

Preparation time: approx. 50 minutes
Per serving: approx. 202 kcal/848 kj, 5 g P, 12 g F, 17 g C

Plum Slices

FOR 24 SERVINGS:

160 ml/5½ fl oz milk
400 g/14 oz plain wheat flour
30 g/1 oz fresh yeast
60 g/2 oz butter
40 g/1½ oz sugar
A pinch of salt
1 egg
1 egg yolk
1 kg/2 lbs 3 oz plums
2 tsp cinnamon powder
3 tbsp vanilla sugar

A pinch of clove powder

200 g/7 oz sour cream

200 g/7 oz crème fraîche

Icing sugar, to decorate

1. Heat the milk in a saucepan. Sift the flour into a bowl, make a hollow in the middle and crumble the yeast into it. Pour the milk over it. Knead everything together and leave to rise in a warm place for approx. 20 minutes.

2. Knead in the butter, sugar, salt, egg and egg yolk. Roll everything into a ball and cover leaving to rise further until the dough has doubled its volume.

3. Preheat the oven to 200 °C/ 390 °F/gas mark 6. Wash and dry the plums, cut in half and remove the stones. Place in a bowl and mix with the cinnamon powder, vanilla sugar and clove powder. Stir the sour cream and crème fraîche into this.

4. Roll the dough out and place onto a greaseproof paper covered baking tray. Cover with the plums and press them gently into the dough.

5. Place on the middle shelf of the oven and bake for approx. 30 minutes. 10 minutes before the end of the baking time, brush the top of the cake with the cream mix and

then finish baking. Sprinkle with icing sugar before serving.

Preparation time: approx. 50 minutes
Per serving: approx. 162 kcal/681 kj,
3 g P, 45 g F, 108 g C

Step 2

Upside Down Apple Pie

FOR 4 SERVINGS:

250 g/9 oz flaky pastry (frozen)

300 g/10¹/₂ oz apples

2 tbsp lemon juice

100 g/3¹/₂ oz sugar

Butter, to grease the baking tin

150 g/5 oz strawberries, to decorate

1. Roll the sheets of pastry on a flour-covered working surface and cut out 4 x 12 cm/4³/₄ in round pieces.

2. Wash the apples and peel them and remove the core with an apple corer. Slice into wedges and sprinkle with lemon juice.

3. Take a 12 cm/4³/₄ in pan and in turn take ¹/₄ of the sugar and heat it to make caramel and then take ¹/₄ of the apples and dip them. Preheat the oven to 180 °C/355 °F/gas mark 4.

4. Cover the pan with one of the pastry pieces.

5. Bake the 4 small caked on the middle shelf of the oven for approx. 10 minutes.

6. Leave the cake to cool for approx. 30 minutes. Then turn upside down, garnish with some strawberries and serve.

Preparation time: approx. 45 minutes
Per serving: approx. 426 kcal/1792 kj,
3 g P, 21 g F, 52 g C

Pear Cake

FOR 24 SERVINGS:

300 g/10¹/₂ oz quark
8 tbsp oil
2 eggs
200 g/7 oz sugar
400 g/14 oz plain wheat flour
¹/₂ tsp baking powder
4 tbsp milk
800 g/1 lb 12 oz pears
3 eggs
¹/₂ tsp cinnamon powder
250 ml/9 fl oz soured milk
2 cl/¹/₂ tsp grape juice
Cinnamon and sugar, to decorate

1. Drain the quark in a sieve and press out gently.

2. Mix the quark together with the oil, eggs, 100 g/3 ¹/₂ oz of the sugar, flour, baking powder and milk and knead into a smooth dough. Preheat the oven to 180 °C/ 355 °F/gas mark 4.

3. Roll the dough out and place onto a greaseproof paper covered baking tray.

4. Wash and dry the pears, peel and cut them in half and remove the cores. Slice into wedges and spread over the dough. Place on the middle shelf of the oven and bake for approx. 30 minutes.

5. Stir together the remaining sugar with the cinnamon powder, soured milk and grape juice.

6. 10 minutes before completion of the baking time, brush the mixture onto the top of the cake and complete baking. Decorate with cinnamon powder and sugar.

Preparation time: approx. 50 min
Per serving: approx.192 kcal/808 kj,
4 g P, 7 g F, 23 g C

Baking with Berries

Blueberries, blackberries and more –
the taste of summer
wrapped in crisp pastry

Blueberry Slices

FOR 8 SERVINGS:

300 g/10¹/₂ oz flaky pastry (frozen)

1 egg whites

50 g/1³/₄ oz marzipan

1 egg

1 egg yolk

30 g/1 oz plain wheat flour

1 tbsp lemon juice

250 g/9 oz large blueberries

2 tbsp pecan nuts

3 tbsp cranberry jam

2 tbsp red wine

Icing sugar, to decorate

1. Roll 2 pieces of the flaky pastry into rectangular strips, each approx. 25 x 12.5 cm/10 x 5 in. Cut along the edges to straighten them out. Preheat the oven to 200 °C/ 390 °F/gas mark 6.

2. Make thin long strips (approx. 1cm/¹/₃ in wide) out of the remaining dough to make sidewalls along the edges of the rectangular portions. Press down gently on the edging so that the frame holds when baked. Brush down all of the dough with the egg white. Puncture the dough base several times with a fork.

3. Place the slices on a baking tray that has been covered with greaseproof paper, and put in the fridge leaving to cool for 30 minutes.

4. Beat together 25 g/1 oz of the marzipan with the eggs until foamy. Stir in the flour and lemon juice. Spread the egg mix on the base of each slice covering it completely.

5. Wash and dry the blueberries, and spread over the egg base of each of the slices. Knead together the remaining marzipan and the coarsely chopped pecan nuts. Crumble over the blueberry layer. Place on the middle shelf of the oven and bake for 15 minutes.

6. Heat the cranberry jam together with the red wine in a saucepan and brush this onto the ready baked slices. Sprinkle with icing sugar and serve.

Preparation time: approx. 45 minutes
Per serving: approx. 265 kcal/1116 kj,
4,5 g P, 15 g L, 22 g G

Raspberry Meringue

FOR 12 SERVINGS:

150 g/5 oz plain wheat flour

A pinch of salt

100 g/3½ oz soft butter

250 g/9 oz sugar

1 egg yolk

1 tbsp vanilla sugar

Butter, to grease baking tin

800 g/1 lb 12 oz raspberries

3 tbsp ginger jam

1 tbsp lemon juice

4 tbsp cornflour

3 egg whites

1. Mix the salt together with the butter, 50 g/1¾ oz of the sugar, 1 egg yolk and the vanilla sugar in a bowl and knead into a smooth dough. Roll the dough into a ball, wrap in cling film and leave in the fridge for an hour. Preheat the oven to 200 °C/390 °F/gas mark 6.

2. Grease a 28 cm/11 in baking tin with butter and sprinkle with some flour. Roll out the dough on a flour-covered working surface and then line the baking tin with it.

3. Press the dough against the outer ring and edges and puncture the base several times with a fork. Place on the middle shelf of the oven and bake for approx. 10 minutes.

4. Trim, wash and dry the raspberries. Place in a saucepan with the lemon juice and jam and heat up gently.

5. Mix the cornflour with a little water, stirring it until it thickens and then add this to the raspberries.

6. Whisk the egg white until stiff and then gradually sprinkle over with the sugar. Spoon the raspberries onto the cake base and spread the meringue mix on top. Place on the middle shelf of the oven and bake at 175 °C/350 °F/gas mark 3–4 for approx. 20 minutes.

Preparation time: approx. 45 minutes
Per serving: approx. 272 kcal/1144 kj,
3 g P, 11 g L, 36 g G

Bilberry Cake

FOR 12 SERVINGS:

400 g/14 oz plain wheat flour

A pinch of salt

4 eggs

150 g/5 oz sugar

250 g/9 oz butter

Butter, to grease the baking tin

$^1/_2$ tsp vanilla extract

200 g/7 oz quark

100 g/3$^1/_2$ oz sour cream

4 tbsp milk

1 tsp cornflour

400 g/14 oz bilberries

1. Add 250 g/9 oz of the flour, salt, one egg, 50 g/1$^3/_4$ oz of the sugar, 100 ml/3$^1/_2$ fl oz water and 170 g/5$^1/_2$ oz of the butter to a mixing bowl and knead into a smooth dough. Roll the dough into a ball, wrap in cling film and leave in the fridge for an hour.

2. Preheat the oven to 200 °C/ 390 °F/gas mark 6. Grease a 24 cm/9$^1/_2$ in springform baking tin with some butter.

3. Take $^2/_3$ of the dough and roll it out on a flour-covered working surface and then line the base of the baking tin with it. Place on the middle shelf of the oven and pre-bake for approx. 15 minutes.

4. Make some edging with the remaining dough and press onto the base once it has cooled down.

5. Separate the rest of the eggs. Whisk the egg white until it is stiff. Stir together the vanilla extract, egg yolk, quark, sour cream, milk and cornflour in a bowl.

6. Wash the bilberries and fold them and the whisked egg snow into the quark mix.

7. Turn the whole mix carefully onto the pre-baked base.

8. Rub the remaining flour, sugar and butter together into a crumble and sprinkle this on top of the fruit quark mix. Place on the middle shelf of the oven and bake for approx. 50 minutes. Allow to cool in the baking tin. Release the edge of the baking tin and remove carefully, transfer to cake plate and serve.

Preparation time: approx. 1 hour
Per serving: approx. 416 kcal/1747 kj,
8 g P, 24 g L, 37 g G

Strawberry Cream Tartlets

FOR 8 SERVINGS:

4 sheets flaky pastry (frozen)

300 g/10½ oz strawberries

2 tbsp orange juice

3 tbsp icing sugar

250 g/9 oz whipping cream

2 tbsp vanilla sugar

2 tbsp apple jam

1. Preheat the oven to 220 °C/ 430 °F/gas mark 7. Cut the pastry into 8 long rectangles and place onto a greaseproof paper covered baking tray. Puncture several times with a fork. Place on the middle shelf of the oven and bake for approx. 12 minutes until the dough starts to bubble up.

2. Wash and dry the strawberries, add to a saucepan together with the orange juice and icing sugar and heat up. When cooked through press through a sieve.

3. Whisk the cream and the vanilla sugar until it is stiff. Slice each pastry in two to use one half as a lid.

4. Spread the apple jam onto the pastry base and then spoon the cream on top of this. Dribble the strawberry sauce over the cream and finish off by placing the pastry lid on top and then serve.

Preparation time: approx. 1 hour
Per serving: approx. 268 kcal/1126 kj,
2,5 g P, 18 g L, 20 g G

Step 1

Step 4

Colourful Berry Cake

FOR 24 SERVINGS:

160 ml/5½ fl oz milk
500 g/1 lb 2 oz plain wheat flour
30 g/1 oz fresh yeast
110 g/4 oz butter
40 g/1½ oz sugar
A pinch of salt
1 egg
1 egg yolk
20 g/¾ oz icing sugar
1 tsp cinnamon powder
375 g/13 oz redcurrants
375 g/13 oz blackberries

1. Heat the milk in a saucepan. Sift 400 g/14 oz of the flour into a bowl, make a hollow in the middle and crumble the yeast into it. Pour the milk over it. Knead everything together and leave to rise in a warm place for approx. 20 minutes. Knead in 60 g/2 oz of the butter, sugar, salt, egg and egg yolk. Roll everything into a ball and cover leaving to rise further until the dough has doubled its volume.

2. Add the remaining flour, butter, icing sugar and cinnamon powder to a bowl and rub together until it forms a crumble. Wash the redcurrants and blackberries separately from each other and dry them out.

3. Preheat the oven to 200 °C/ 390 °F/gas mark 6. Roll the dough out and place onto a greaseproof paper covered baking tray.

4. Cut a cross through the dough to separate the base into 4 rectangles.

Spread the redcurrants and black-berries alternately on each rectangle to make a chequered pattern. Sprinkle the crumble over the fruit and then place on the middle shelf of the oven and bake for 35 minutes.

Preparation time: approx. 45 minutes (excluding standing time) Per serving: approx. 139 kcal/585 kj, 3 g P, 5 g L, 106 g G

Step 1

Cranberry Snow Cake

FOR 12 SERVINGS:

100 g/3½ oz butter

200 g/7 oz sugar

1 tbsp vanilla sugar

1 egg

175 g/6 oz plain flour

1 tsp baking powder

A pinch of salt

Butter, to grease baking tin

50 g/1¾ oz nut flakes

400 g/14 oz cranberries

2 egg whites

1. Cream the butter in a bowl. Stir in 80 g/2¾ oz of the sugar, the vanilla sugar and 1 egg. Preheat the oven to 200 °C/390 °F/gas mark 6.

2. Mix the flour together with the baking powder and salt and then fold into the butter mix. Grease a 24 cm/9½ in springform baking tin. Spoon the dough mix into the tin.

3. Sprinkle the base with the nuts. Wash and dry the cranberries and spread them over the dough evenly. Sprinkle over 20 g/¾ oz of the sugar.

4. Place on the middle shelf of the oven and bake for approx. 30 minutes.

5. Whisk the egg white with the rest of the sugar until it is stiff. Fill into a icing bag and decorate the cake with cream whirls. Bake the cake for a further 15 minutes or until golden brown.

Preparation time: approx. 1 hour
Per serving: approx. 250 kcal/1048 kj,
3 g P, 9 g L, 35 g G

Step 5

Gooseberry Cake

FOR 24 SERVINGS:

300 g/10½ oz plain wheat flour

125 g/4½ oz sugar

A pinch of salt

1 heaped tbsp baking powder

1 egg yolk

175 g/6 oz lard

750 g/1 lb 11 oz gooseberries

100 g/3½ oz maple syrup

Butter, to grease baking tray

Icing sugar, to decorate

1. Mix the flour, sugar, lard, salt, baking powder and egg yolk together in a bowl and then knead into a smooth dough. Roll the dough into a ball, wrap in cling film and leave in the fridge for an hour. Preheat the oven to 200 °C/ 390 °F/gas mark 6.

2. Wash and dry the gooseberries. Add to a saucepan together with the maple syrup and heat gently for 3 minutes.

3. Roll the dough onto a lightly flour-covered working surface, making it slightly larger than the baking tray. Place on the baking tray and cover with the gooseberries and syrup.

4. Using your fingers to press the edge of the dough up to make an edge. Place on the middle shelf of the oven and bake for approx. 45 minutes. Sprinkle with icing sugar before serving.

Preparation time: approx. 1 hour
Per serving: approx. 177 kcal/744 kj,
2 g P, 8 g L, 22 g G

Blackberry Cake

FOR 12 SERVINGS:

300 g/10½ oz plain wheat flour

225 g/8 oz butter

1 tbsp milk

210 g/7½ oz sugar

3 egg yolks

A pinch of salt

A pinch of baking powder

600 g/1 lb 5 oz blackberries

200 g/7 oz rhubarb

7 tbsp blackberry liqueur

180 g/6½ oz chocolate flakes

50 g/1¾ oz ground hazelnuts

Butter, to grease baking tin

2 tbsp breadcrumbs

1. Mix 250 g/9 oz of the flour, 125 g/4½ oz of the butter, 60 g/2 oz of the sugar, salt, baking powder and 2 egg yolks together in a bowl and knead into a smooth dough. Roll the dough into a ball, wrap in cling film and leave in the fridge for an hour.

2. Trim, wash and dry the blackberries. Trim, wash and dry the rhubarb as well, peeling if necessary and then chop into 3 cm/1¼ in pieces. Place the fruit in a large bowl and stir in the blackberry liqueur, chocolate flakes and 60 g/2 oz of the sugar. Leave to draw for approx. 30 minutes.

3. Preheat the oven to 200 °C/390 °F/gas mark 6. Rub together the remaining flour, butter, sugar, one egg yolk and the hazelnut until it becomes a fine crumble.

4. Roll 2/3 of the dough on a flour-covered working surface into a cycle approx. 26 cm/10 in. Take a 26 cm/10 in springform baking tin, grease with butter and line with the dough. Puncture the base several times with a fork and place on the middle shelf of the oven and pre-bake for approx. 10 minutes.

5. Drain the fruit completely. Make a rim with the remaining dough and then sprinkle breadcrumbs onto the pre-baked base.

6. Spoon the fruit onto the dough, and sprinkle over with the crumble. Place the blackberry cake on the middle shelf of the oven and bake for approx. 45 minutes.

Preparation time: approx. 45 minutes (excluding standing time)
Per serving: approx. 422 kcal/1775 kj, 5,5 g P, 21 g L, 48 g G

Step 4

Franconian Gooseberry Flan

FOR 24 SERVINGS:

160 ml/5¹/₂ fl oz milk

500 g/1 lb 2 oz plain wheat flour

30 g/1 oz fresh yeast

110 g/4 oz butter

100 g/3¹/₂ oz sugar

A pinch of salt

1 egg

1 egg yolk

20 g/³/₄ oz icing sugar

100 g/3¹/₂ oz almond pieces

750 g/1 lb 11 oz green and red goose-berries

Decorating sugar

1. Heat the milk in a saucepan. Sift 400 g/14 oz of the flour into a bowl, make a hollow in the middle and crumble the yeast into it. Pour the milk over it. Knead everything together and leave to rise in a warm place for approx. 20 minutes.

2. Mix 40 g/1¹/₂ oz of the sugar, 60 g/2 oz of the butter, salt, egg and egg yolk together in a bowl and knead into a smooth dough. Roll everything into a ball and cover leaving to rise further until the dough has doubled its volume.

3. Rub the remaining flour and butter with the icing sugar in a bowl, kneading slightly until it forms a crumble.

4. Wash and dry the gooseberries. Preheat the oven to 200 °C/390 °F/gas mark 6. Cover a baking tray with greaseproof paper and roll the dough onto it.

5. Cover the dough with a layer of gooseberries and sprinkle over the remaining sugar and almond pieces. Now cover wit the crumble mix and place on the middle shelf of the oven and bake for approx. 35 minutes. Garnish with decorating sugar and serve.

Preparation time: approx. 45 minutes
Per serving: approx. 149 kcal/621 kj,
24 g P, 44 g L, 150 g G

Step 3

Warm Fruit Pasties

FOR 12 PASTIES:

300 g/10½ oz flaky pastry
400 g/14 oz strawberries
100 g/3½ oz pineapple chunks (tinned)
200 g/7 oz cream cheese
2 cl/½ tsp white rum
1 tbsp lemon juice
2 egg yolks
Icing sugar, to decorate

1. Roll the flaky pastry out onto a lightly flour-covered working sur face and cut into 12 rectangles (approx. 15 x 12 cm/6 x 4³/4 in).

2. Wash and dry the strawberries and chop into small pieces. Drain the pineapple chunks.

3. Preheat the oven to 180 °C/ 355 °F/gas mark 4. Stir the cream cheese, rum and lemon juice together. Fold in the strawberry and pineapple pieces.

4. Whisk the egg yolk in a bowl. Turn 3 tablespoons of the cheese-fruit mix onto one half of each pastry base. Brush the edges of the dough with the egg yolk and fold the empty half over, pressing down the edges to seal using the back of a fork.

3. Put the small pasties on a greaseproof paper covered baking tray and place on the middle shelf of the oven and bake for approx. 30 minutes. Sprinkle with icing sugar before serving.

Preparation time: approx. 50 minutes
Per serving: approx. 180 kcal/754 kj, 4 g P, 12 g L, 10 g G

Redcurrant Cream Puffs

FOR 12 PUFFS:

50 g/1¾ oz butter

A pinch of salt

150 g/5 oz plain wheat flour

4 eggs

2 tbsp sugar

1 tbsp hazelnut flakes

1 tbsp almond flakes

250 g/9 oz crème fraîche

150 g/5 oz cream yoghurt

2 tbsp lemon juice

80 g/2¾ oz icing sugar

6 leaves of white gelatine

600 g/1 lb 5 oz redcurrants

2 tbsp redcurrant liqueur

4 tbsp redcurrant jam

Icing sugar, to decorate

1. Add the butter to 250 ml/9 fl oz water in a saucepan and bring to the boil. Preheat the oven to 200 °C/390 °F/gas mark 6.

2. Add the salt and flour to this stirring the mixture well until a smooth clump forms. Put the clump in a bowl and knead in the eggs one after the other.

3. Prepare a baking tray with greaseproof paper and spoon small portions of dough onto it, each approx. 5 cm/2 in apart. Sprinkle with the sugar, hazelnut flakes and almond flakes. Place on the middle shelf of the oven and bake for approx. 35 minutes.

4. Mix the crème fraîche together with the yoghurt, lemon juice and icing sugar. Place the gelatine in cold water to soak and let it dissolve.

5. Remove the puffs from the oven and cut them in half immediately. Stir 2 tablespoons cream mix into the gelatine and then in turn fold this into the rest of the cream mix.

6. Wash the redcurrants, remove the stalks and allow to dry.

7. Mix together the redcurrants with the liqueur and jam , heat up gently in a saucepan and allow to draw briefly.

8. Spoon the redcurrants onto the lower puff and add the cream on top. Place the upper puff half on top of the filling and put in a cool place, until the cream is stiff. Decorate with icing sugar and serve.

Preparation time: approx. 50 minutes
Per serving: approx. 273 kcal/1146 kj,
5,5 g P, 14 g L, 6 g G

Gooseberry Yoghurt Cake

FOR 12 SERVINGS:

170 g/5¹/₂ oz plain wheat flour

A pinch of salt

¹/₂ tbsp baking powder

60 g/2 oz sugar

1–2 drops vanilla extract

65 g/2 oz butter

Butter, to grease baking tin

500 g/1 lb 2 oz gooseberries (preserved)

3 tbsp cake glaze

200 g/7 oz low fat yoghurt

200 g/7 oz sour cream

8 leaves of white gelatine

250 ml/9 fl oz whipping cream

20 g/³/₄ oz chopped hazelnuts

1. Mix the salt, baking powder, sugar, vanilla extract and butter together and knead into a dough.

2. Grease a 24 cm/9¹/₂ in spring-form baking tin and line with the dough. Puncture the base several times with a fork. Leave in a cool place for 30 minutes. Place the tin in a cold oven and then turn on bringing the temperature up to 200 °C/390 °F/gas mark 6, baking then for a further 20 minutes.

3. Drain the gooseberries and pour onto the pre-baked cake base. Prepare the cake glaze as instructed on the packaging and pour over the fruit.

4. Mix the sour cream with the yoghurt. Place the gelatine in water to dissolve and then stir the yoghurt mix into it.

5. Whisk the cream until it is stiff and carefully fold it into the yoghurt mix. Spoon over the gooseberries and sprinkle with the chopped hazelnuts. Allow to harden then serve.

Preparation time: approx. 50 minutes
Per serving: approx. 262 kcal/1101 kj,
3,5 g P, 16 g L, 22 g G

Step 4

Step 5

The Kings Blackberry Cake

FOR 12 SERVINGS:

100 g/3½ oz soft butter
100 g/3½ oz sugar
1 tbsp vanilla sugar
2 eggs
175 g/6 oz plain wheat flour
15 g/½ oz cocoa powder
A pinch of salt
1 tbsp baking powder
6 tbsp milk
300 g/10½ oz blackberries
3 leaves of red gelatine
200 g/7 oz whipping cream
2 tbsp blackberry jam
150 g/5 oz icing sugar
2 tsp lemon juice
4 tbsp chopped pistachios
12 green marzipan leaves

1. Preheat the oven to 180 °C/ 355 °F/gas mark 4. Heat the butter in a saucepan and stir until creamy, adding the sugar, vanilla sugar and eggs bit by bit. Keep stirring until everything dissolves into a creamy substance. Sift the flour, cocoa powder, salt and baking powder into a bowl. Add this flour mix and the milk alternately to the butter cream slowly stirring in.

2. Line a 30 cm/12 in long loaf tin with the dough mix and smooth off the top. Place on the middle shelf of the oven and bake for approx. 55 minutes.

3. Take the cake out of the oven, turn it out of the tin and leave to cool. Trim, wash and dry the black-berries, laying some to the side for decoration later.

4. Take the blackberries and press them through a sieve. Soak the gelatine in a pan with cold water. Whisk the cream until it is stiff and fold into the blackberry mix. Squeeze out the gelatine and dissolve over a low heat. Add some of the blackberry mixture to the gelatine, stirring it well, then gently fold into the rest of the blackberry cream.

5. Cut the cake horizontally into three layers. Spread the black-berry jam onto two of the slices followed by the cream on each layer. Place the slices on top of each other again and leave to cool for 30 minutes. Stir together the icing sugar, lemon juice and remaining blackberry paste and brush the top of the cake with it. Decorate with the chopped pistachios, marzipan leaves and the last of the blackberries.

Preparation time: approx. 1 ½ hour (excluding standing time)
Per serving: approx. 316 kcal/1327 kj, 4 g P, 14 g L, 40 g G

Colourful Fruits of the Forest Cake

FOR 8 SERVINGS:

150 g/5 oz plain wheat flour

A pinch of salt

3 tbsp oil

400 g/14 oz mixed fruits of the forest (frozen)

Juice and rind of 1 untreated lemon

2 tbsp vanilla sugar

3 tbsp sugar

80 g/2³/4 oz marzipan paste

60 g/2 oz butter

Butter, to grease the baking tin

Berries, to garnish

Icing sugar, to decorate

1. Mix the flour with the salt, oil and 80 ml/2³/4 fl oz water and knead into a dough. Leave to stand for 1 hour. Preheat the oven to 200 °C/390 °F/gas mark 6.

2. Mix the berries in a bowl with the lemon juice, lemon rind, vanilla sugar, sugar and 50 g/1³/4 oz of the marzipan paste.

3. Melt the butter in a saucepan. Grease a 22 cm/8³/4 in springform baking tin with butter.

4. Roll the dough into a round shape and line the tin with it, pulling on the edges to make it overlap the sides of the baking tin at least 10 cm/4 in.

5. Fill with the fruit. Fold the excess dough over and inwards, leaving a hole in the middle of the cake.

6. Brush the dough with the melted butter and cover the top with greaseproof paper. Place on the middle shelf of the oven and bake for approx. 20 minutes.

7. Remove the paper and brush again with the melted butter. Bake for about another 20 minutes. Crumble the marzipan over the top of the cake and sprinkle the rest of the butter over it. Bake a further 5 minutes again on the middle shelf. Garnish with some fresh berries and Sprinkle with icing sugar and serve.

Preparation time: approx. 45 minutes
Per serving: approx. 252 kcal/1058 kj,
3,5 g P, 14 g L, 24 g G

Raspberry Quark Flan

FOR 24 SERVINGS:

300 g/10½ oz plain wheat flour

200 g/7 oz butter, chopped

250 g/9 oz sugar

Salt

¼ rind of 1 untreated lemon

4 eggs

100 g/3½ oz raspberries

3 tbsp raspberry liqueur

A few drops of vanilla extract

1 kg/2 lbs 3 oz cream quark

2 tbsp cornflour

50 g/1¾ oz desiccated coconut

Icing sugar, to decorate

Fresh lemon balm, to garnish

1. Add the flour, butter pieces, 100 g/3½ oz of the sugar, salt, lemon rind and an egg to a working surface and chop up finely. Knead all the ingredients together and roll the resulting dough into a ball, wrap in cling film and leave to stand for 1 hour in a cool place. Preheat the oven to 200 °C/390 °F/ gas mark 6.

2. Trim, wash and dry the raspberries and sprinkle with the raspberry liqueur. Leave to draw for approx. 10 minutes.

3. Separate the rest of the eggs, and whisk the egg yolks with the vanilla extract and remaining sugar until light and foamy. Drain the quark and fold, together with the cornflour, in to the egg mix. Then carefully fold in the raspberries.

4. Whisk the egg white until it is stiff and gently fold it into the quark mix.

5. Roll the dough out and place onto a greaseproof paper covered baking tray. Sprinkle with the coconut. Spread with the quark cream and place on the middle shelf of the oven and bake for approx. 30 minutes. Sprinkle with icing sugar and garnish with the lemon balm before serving.

Preparation time: approx. 45 minutes
Per serving: approx. 304 kcal/1276 kj,
37 g P, 86 g L, 123 g G

Cranberry Tart

FOR 12 SERVINGS:

250 g/9 oz plain wheat flour

50 g/1¾ oz sugar

A pinch of salt

100 g/3½ oz cold butter, chopped

300 g/10½ oz peanuts

250 g/9 oz cranberries

200 ml/7 fl oz grape juice

85 g/3 oz soft butter

3 eggs

40 g/1½ oz brown sugar

80 g/2¾ oz white sugar

Butter, to grease the pie dish

Icing sugar

1. Mix the flour with the sugar and salt. Add the cold butter pieces to the flour and knead, then chop the dough up finely.

2. Add 2–3 tablespoons of cold water and knead into the dough. Roll the dough into a ball, wrap in cling film and leave to stand for 1 hour in a cool place.

3. Preheat the oven to 175 °C/ 350 °F/gas mark 3–4. Coarsely chop the peanuts. Wash and dry the cranberries and put in a saucepan with the grape juice. Heat gently for approx. 5 minutes.

4. Remove from the heat and drain. Melt 85 g/3 oz butter in a saucepan. Mix the brown and white sugar with the eggs and stir

until everything is dissolved and creamy.

5. Fold in the melted butter, peanuts and cranberries.

6. Roll the dough out onto a flour-covered working surface. Take a 26 cm/10 in pie dish and grease with butter. Line with the dough. Add the filling, spread evenly and smooth over.

7. Place on the middle shelf of the oven and bake for approx. 40 minutes. Turn out of the pie dish and leave to cool. Sprinkle with icing sugar before serving.

Preparation time: approx. 1 hour
Per serving: approx. 450 kcal/1887 kj,
10 g P, 26 g L, 36 g G

Step 5

81

Blackberry Mascarpone Cake

FOR 24 SERVINGS:

160 ml/5¹/₂ fl oz milk
400 g/14 oz plain wheat flour
30 g/1 oz fresh yeast
60 g/2 oz butter
40 g/1¹/₂ oz sugar
A pinch of salt
5 eggs
1 egg yolk
750 g/1 lb 11 oz blackberries
200 g/7 oz marzipan paste
500 g/1 lb 2 oz Mascarpone
2 tbsp vanilla sugar
2 packets (6 heaped tbsp) vanilla pudding powder
2 tbsp blackberry liqueur

1. Heat the milk in a saucepan. Sift the flour into a bowl, make a hollow in the middle and crumble the yeast into it. Pour the milk over it. Knead everything together and leave to rise in a warm place for approx. 20 minutes.

2. Knead in the butter, sugar, salt, 1 egg and egg yolk. Roll everything into a ball and cover leaving to rise further until the dough has doubled its volume.

3. Trim, wash and dry the blackberries. Preheat the oven to 200 °C/390 °F/gas mark 6.

4. Roll the dough out and place onto a greaseproof paper covered baking tray. Crumble the marzipan into a bowl and add the remaining eggs, Mascarpone, vanilla sugar and pudding powder stirring until smooth. Mix in the blackberry liqueur.

5. Cover the dough with the blackberries and brush over with the cheese cream mix. Place on the middle shelf of the oven and bake for approx. 30 minutes.

Preparation time: approx. 1 hour
Per serving: approx. 231 kcal/970 kj,
2 g P, 8 g L, 12 g G

Fruity Tarts

FOR 10 TARTS:

250 ml/9 fl oz milk

Few drops vanilla extract

50 g/1³/₄ oz sugar

20 g/³/₄ oz vanilla pudding powder

2 egg yolks

30 g/1 oz marzipan paste

2 tbsp Amaretto

500 g/1 lb 2 oz raspberries

10 short crust pastry tartlets
(ready-made)

3 tbsp cake glaze

2 tbsp sugar

250 ml/9 fl oz red wine

50 g/1³/₄ oz chopped hazelnuts

Mint, to garnish

1. Add the milk, leaving a little for later, to a saucepan with the vanilla extract and bring to the boil. Add 25 g/1 oz of the sugar.

2. Mix the remaining sugar, pudding powder, egg yolk and remaining milk in a bowl and then add to the milk in the saucepan.

3. Bring again to the boil, stirring continuously and leave to draw. Add the marzipan. Fill into a cold container.

4. Add the Amaretto. Wash and dry the raspberries. Put 1 table-spoon of the cream mix into each tartlet and cover with raspberries. Prepare the cake glaze according to instructions and add the red wine and sugar to it. Pour over the raspberries. Sprinkle with the hazelnuts, garnish with the mint and serve.

Preparation time: approx. 1 hour
(excluding standing time)
Per serving: approx. 202 kcal/849 kj,
5 g P, 7 g L, 22 g G

Step 1

Step 2

Strawberry Biscuit Omelettes

For 8 servings:

5 egg yolks

110 g/4 oz sugar

A pinch of salt

Grated rind of 1/2 an untreated lemon

4 egg whites

70 g/2 1/2 oz plain flour

40 g/1 1/2 oz cornflour

40 g/1 1/2 oz warm butter

200 g/7 oz strawberries

250 g/9 oz quark

50 ml/1 3/4 fl oz strawberry syrup

1 tbsp vanilla sugar

1. Whisk the egg yolk with 30 g/ 1 oz sugar until foamy and light. Add the salt and lemon rind. Preheat the oven to 200 °C/390 °F/ gas mark 6.

2. Whisk the egg white with the remaining sugar until it is stiff, and then carefully fold it into the egg yolk mix. Sift the flour and corn-flour and slowly stir it in.

3. Finally fold in the warm butter very carefully. Fill everything into an icing bag, and make 10 cm/4 in round flat cakes on a greaseproof paper covered baking tray.

4. Place on the middle shelf of the oven and bake for approx. 10 minutes.

5. Wash and dry the strawberries and cut into wedges. Mix the quark, syrup and vanilla sugar. Stir in the strawberries. Take the omelettes out of the oven dress with the strawberry cream and serve.

Preparation time: approx. 1 hour
Per serving: approx. 295 kcal/1240 kj,
8 g P, 14 g L, 31 g G

Fruity Sponge Cake

FOR 24 SERVINGS:

300 g/10¹/₂ oz plain wheat flour

200 g/7 oz butter, chopped

250 g/9 oz sugar

Salt

¹/₄ tsp grated rind of 1 untreated lemon

1 egg

100 g/3¹/₂ oz raspberries

100 g/3¹/₂ oz blackberries

100 g/3¹/₂ oz bilberries

5 tbsp lemon juice

5 egg whites

1. Mix flour with the butter pieces, 100 g/3¹/₂ oz sugar, salt, lemon rind and an egg, then chop up finely on a working surface. Knead together again and roll into a ball, wrap in cling film and leave to stand for an hour in a cool place. Preheat the oven to 200 °C/390 °F/ gas mark 6.

2. Trim, wash and dry the raspberries, blackberries and bilberries and sprinkle with lemon juice. Leave to draw for 10 minutes.

3. Roll the dough out onto a flour-covered working surface and place on a greaseproof paper covered baking tray. Place on the middle shelf of the oven and bake for approx. 25 minutes.

4. Whisk the egg white with the remaining sugar until it is stiff. Distribute the berries onto the dough and spread the egg mix on top. Bake again on the middle shelf for approx. 10 minutes.

Preparation time: approx. 1 hour
Per serving: approx. 239 kcal/1006 kj,
3,5 g P, 11 g L, 29 g G

Step 1

Step 4

Fruits of the Forest Flan

FOR 24 SERVINGS:

300 g/10½ oz plain wheat flour

200 g/7 oz butter, chopped

100 g/3½ oz sugar

A pinch of salt

½ tsp grated rind of 1 untreated lemon

1 egg

1 tsp gingerbread spices

500 g/1 lb 2 oz fruits of the forest (frozen)

3 tbsp lemon juice

1 tbsp rum

7 cashew nuts

200 g/7 oz chocolate coating

Icing sugar, to decorate

1. Add flour, butter pieces, sugar, salt, lemon rind, egg and ginger-bread spices onto a working sur-face and chop up finely. Then knead it all together. Roll the dough into a ball, wrap in cling film and leave to stand for an hour in a cool place. Preheat the oven to 200 °C/390 °F/gas mark 6.

2. Sprinkle the rum and lemon juice over the berries and leave to draw for 5 minutes.

3. Roll the dough onto a flour-covered working surface, and then lay on a greaseproof paper covered baking tray. Cover with the berries. Place on the middle shelf of the oven and bake for approx. 10 minutes.

4. Melt the chocolate coating in a water bath and decorate the tray slice with it. Garnish with cashew nuts and Sprinkle with icing sugar before serving.

Preparation time: approx. 1 hours
Per serving: approx. 171 kcal/721 kj,
2 g P, 8 g L, 20 g G

Fruity Bagels

FOR 24 BAGELS:

160 ml/5¹/₂ fl oz milk

400 g/14 oz plain wheat flour

30 g/1 oz fresh yeast

60 g/2 oz butter

40 g/1¹/₂ oz sugar

A pinch of salt

1 egg

2 egg yolks

3 tbsp raspberry jam

3 tbsp blackberry jam

3 tbsp gooseberry jam

30 g/1 oz almond pieces

30 g/1 oz decorating sugar

30 g/1 oz hazelnut flakes

Berries, to garnish

1. Heat the milk in a saucepan. Sift the flour into a bowl, make a hollow in the middle and crumble the yeast into it. Pour the milk over it. Knead everything together and leave to rise in a warm place for approx. 20 minutes.

2. Knead in the butter, sugar, salt, 1 egg and egg yolk. Roll everything into a ball and cover leaving to rise further until the dough has doubled its volume.

3. Roll the dough out on a flour-covered working surface. Cut out round shapes and use to line small (Savarin) tart moulds.

4. Brush the tops with the remaining egg yolk and place on the middle shelf of the oven and bake for approx. 25 minutes.

5. Turn the ready bagels out of the moulds and top each one with a dollop on one of the jams. Garnish alternately with the berries, almond pieces, hazelnut flakes and decorating sugar and serve.

Preparation time: approx. 45 minutes
Per serving: approx. 121 kcal/508 kj,
3 g P, 4 g L, 15 g G

Juicy Bilberry Slices

FOR 24 SERVINGS:

250 g/9 oz flaky pastry (frozen)
900 g/2 lb bilberries
50 ml/1¾ fl oz crème de cassis
3 tbsp lemon juice
100 g/3½ oz butter
Icing sugar, to decorate

1. Defrost flaky pastry and then roll onto a flour-covered working surface to the size of your baking tray.

2. Preheat the oven to 220 °C/ 430 °F/gas mark 7. Cover your baking tray with greaseproof paper and lay the dough onto it.

3. Wash and dry the bilberries. Add half of the berries to a saucepan together with the crème de cassis and lemon juice. Heat up gently and allow to draw for approx. 4 minutes.

4. While still warm pour the bilberries onto the dough base and add the remaining bilberries too.

5. Put chunks of butter onto the berries and Place on the middle shelf of the oven and bake for approx. 15 minutes. Sprinkle with icing sugar before serving.

Preparation time: approx. 45 minutex
Per serving: approx. 105 kcal/443 kj,
2 g P, 7 g L, 6 g G

Cranberry Slices

FOR 24 SERVINGS:

800 g/1 lb 12 oz quark
8 tbsp oil
2 eggs
200 g/7 oz sugar
400 g/14 oz plain wheat flour
½ tsp baking powder
4 tbsp milk
500 g/1 lb 2 oz redcurrants
6 tbsp redcurrant jam
2 tbsp Grappa
40 g/1½ oz desiccated coconut
2 tbsp vanilla sugar

6 tbsp lemon juice

Grated rind of ¹/₂ an untreated lemon

6 leaves of white gelatine

1. Drain 300 g/10¹/₂ oz of the quark through a sieve and press out excess liquid. Preheat the oven to 180 °C/355 °F/gas mark 4.

2. Mix the quark with the oil, eggs, 100 g/3¹/₂ oz of the sugar, flour, baking powder and milk and knead into a smooth dough.

3. Roll the dough out and place onto a greaseproof paper covered baking tray. Place on the middle shelf of the oven and bake for approx. 30 minutes.

4. Wash and dry the redcurrants. Gently heat up the cranberry jam

and Grappa in a saucepan and brush onto the ready baked dough base.

5. Spread the redcurrants and coconut onto the dough.

6. Mix the vanilla sugar with 500 g/ 1 lb 2 oz of the quark, the rest of the sugar, lemon juice and lemon rind. Soak the gelatine, press out and then dissolve in a little warm water. Stir the gelatine into the quark mix. Brush onto the top of the cake and place in the fridge until everything has hardened.

Preparation time: approx. 50 minutes (excluding standing time)
Per serving: approx. 208 kcal/876 kj, 5 g P, 9 g L, 23 g G

Step 1

Blackberry Quark Cakes

FOR 24 SERVINGS:

300 g/10¹/₂ oz quark

8 tbsp oil

2 eggs

200 g/7 oz sugar

400 g/14 oz plain wheat flour

¹/₂ tsp baking powder

4 tbsp milk

4 egg whites

500 g/1 lb 2 oz blackberries

1. Drain the quark through a sieve and press any excess liquid out gently.

2. Mix the quark with the oil, eggs, 100 g/3¹/₂ oz sugar, flour, baking powder and the milk and knead all together into a smooth dough. Preheat the oven to 180 °C/355 °F/gas mark 4.

3. Cover a baking tray with greaseproof paper and roll the dough onto it.

4. Whisk the egg white until it is stiff and drizzle the rest of the sugar over it.

5. Wash and dry the blackberries and fold into the egg snow mix. Spread onto the dough and place

on the middle shelf of the oven and bake for approx. 30 minutes.

Preparation time: approx. 45 minutes
Per serving: approx. 141 kcal/593 kj,
4 g P, 3 g L, 21 g G

Step 5

Redcurrant Tart

FOR 12 SERVINGS:

100 g/3½ oz soft butter

100 g/3½ oz sugar

1 tbsp vanilla sugar

2 eggs

175 g/6 oz plain wheat flour

A pinch of salt

2 heaped tbsp baking powder

6 tbsp milk

200 g/7 oz cream

1 cl/¼ tsp redcurrant liqueur

1 tbsp redcurrant jam

150 g/5 oz redcurrants

Fresh lemon balm, to garnish

1. Preheat the oven to 180 °C/ 355 °F/gas mark 4. Heat the butter in a saucepan very gently and stir until creamy. Slowly add 100 g/ 3½ oz of the sugar, vanilla sugar and the eggs to it. Stir continuously until the mixture is a fine creamy consistency. Sift the flour, salt and baking powder into a bowl. Fold the flour mix and milk alternately into the dough mix.

2. Line a 26 cm/10 in springform baking tin with the dough and smooth down. Place on the middle shelf of the oven and bake for approx. 55 minutes.

3. Whisk the cream until it is stiff and light. Fold in the redcurrant liqueur and jam.

4. Cut the cake horizontally into 3 equal layers. Remove the redcurrants from the stalks and wash and dry. Spread 1/3 of the cream mix onto each layer of cake, pressing in some redcurrants here and there. Build the layers up and use the rest of the cream and redcurrants for the top. Place in the fridge to harden for approx. 1 hour. Garnish with lemon balm and serve.

Preparation time: approx. 45 minutes (excluding standing time)
Per serving: approx. 221 kcal/928 kj, 4 g P, 13 g L, 21 g G

Light Strawberry Pastries

FOR 24 PASTRIES:

160 ml/5½ fl oz milk

400 g/14 oz plain wheat flour

30 g/1 oz fresh yeast

60 g/2 oz butter

40 g/1½ oz sugar

A pinch of salt

1 egg

2 egg yolk

400 g/14 oz strawberries

80 g/2¾ oz desiccated coconut

100 ml/3 ½ fl oz Genever (Dutch gin)

Milk, to brush over

100 g/3½ oz icing sugar

1 tbsp lemon juice

10 g/⅓ oz butter, melted

1. Heat the milk in a saucepan. Sift the flour into a bowl, make a hollow in the middle and crumble the yeast into it. Pour the milk over it. Knead everything together and leave to rise in a warm place for approx. 20 minutes.

2. Knead in the butter, sugar, salt, egg and egg yolk. Roll everything into a ball and cover leaving to rise further until the dough has doubled its volume. Preheat the oven to 180 °C/355 °F/gas mark 4.

3. Wash and dry the strawberries, cut into wedges. Mix in a bowl with the coconut and sprinkle with the Genever gin.

4. Knead the dough again and roll out onto a flour-covered working surface. Cut out into 12 cm/4¾ in round cake bases. Spread 1 tablespoon of the strawberries onto the middle of each. Brush some milk on the edges and fold each dough circle together, pressing down on the edges. Brush the outside of each pastry with milk and 1 egg yolk and then place on the middle shelf of the oven and bake for approx. 20 minutes.

5. Stir the icing sugar with lemon juice and melted butter and brush onto the pastries shortly before serving.

Preparation time: approx. 45 minutes
Per serving: approx. 95 kcal/401 kj, 13 g P, 37 g L, 42 g G

Strawberry Doughnuts

FOR 12 DOUGHNUTS:

150 g/5 oz plain wheat flour

4 tsp baking powder

75 g/2½ oz low fat quark

50 ml/1¾ fl oz milk

50 ml/1¾ fl oz sunflower oil

40 g/1½ oz sugar

1 tbsp vanilla sugar

Small bottle of butter-vanilla extract

Salt

200 g/7 oz strawberries

15 sugar cubes

Oil for deep frying

Icing sugar, to decorate

1. Mix the flour with the baking powder, quark, milk, oil, sugar, vanilla sugar, butter-vanilla extract and salt and knead into a dough. Roll the dough flat onto a flour-covered working surface and then roll together.

2. Wash and dry the strawberries and cut into pieces. Slice the dough into 12 pieces and fill the middle of each one with some strawberries and a sugar cube. Roll each one into a ball.

3. Heat the oil in a deep fat fryer, and put the dough mix in the oil briefly or until they are golden brown. Take out with a skimmer spoon and leave to drip dry.

4. Sprinkle with icing sugar and serve.

Preparation time: approx. 50 minutes
Per serving: approx. 145 kcal/610 kj,
2 g P, 8 g L, 12 g G

Step 1

Step 2

Exotic Fruit from Around the World

Papaya, lychee, melon and kiwi fruit give your baking that certain holiday feeling. Live and enjoy the dream.

Date Cake with Topping

FOR 12 SERVINGS:

500 g/1 lb 2 oz dates
150 ml/¼ pint white rum
75 g/2½ oz butter
A pinch of salt
1 tbsp vanilla sugar
150 g/5 oz plain wheat flour
½ tsp baking powder
Butter, to grease pie mould
2 egg whites
2 egg yolks
50 g/1¾ oz breadcrumbs
6 tbsp whipping cream

1. Mix the dates and rum in a bowl and leave to marinate for approx. 24 hours.

2. Preheat the oven to 200 °C/ 390 °F/gas mark 6. Mix the sugar, 75 g/2½ oz of the butter, salt, vanilla sugar, flour and baking powder and knead it all together into a smooth dough.

3. Roll the dough into a ball, wrap in cling film and leave to stand in a cool place for approx. 1 hour.

4. Drain the dates. Grease a 26 cm/10 in pie mould with butter. Roll the dough out flat on a flour-covered working surface and line

the mould with it. Press the edges down a little.

5. Place on the middle shelf of the oven and bake for 7 minutes.

6. Whisk the egg white until it is stiff and sprinkle over with the remaining sugar. Fold in the egg yolks, breadcrumbs and cream and the topping is ready. Turn the dates into the pie base and pour over with the egg topping.

7. Place on the middle shelf of the oven and bake for 15 minutes.

Preparation time: approx. 45 minutes
Per serving: approx. 330 kcal/1386 kj,
4 g P, 8 g L, 50 g G

Papaya Cream Puffs

FOR 12 CREAM PUFFS:

100 g/3½ oz butter

150 g/5 oz plain wheat flour

4 eggs

A pinch of salt

1 papaya, approx. 500 g/1 lb 2 oz

100 g/3½ oz sugar

3 tbsp lemon juice

350 g/12 oz Mascarpone

A pinch of cinnamon powder

A pinch of aniseed powder

50 ml/1¾ fl oz coconut milk

250 ml/9 fl oz whipping cream

2 tbsp icing sugar

1. Heat the butter in a saucepan with 250 ml/9 fl oz water and bring to the boil. Sift over with flour, stirring continuously until a doughy clump forms on the floor of the pan. Remove the dough from the heat and leave to cool.

2. Knead the eggs into the dough one after the other and then add salt. Cover and leave to stand in a cool place for approx. 1 hour. Preheat the oven to 200 °C/390 °F/ gas mark 6.

3. Peel the papaya, remove it's stone and cut into thin strips. Sprinkle over with sugar and lemon juice.

4. Cover a baking tray with grease-proof paper. Pour the dough mix into an icing bag with a star nozzle and squeeze out 12 rectangular portions onto the tray, each measuring 4 x 6 cm/1½ x 2½ in.

5. Place on the middle shelf of the oven and bake for 20 minutes.

6. Stir together the Mascarpone, spices, coconut milk and cream. Remove the cream puffs from the oven and immediately cut them in half horizontally and then leave to cool. Fill the cheese-cream mix into an icing bag again with a star-shaped nozzle and squeeze the filling onto the lower half of the puffs. Put the papaya strips on top and top with the upper puff half. Sprinkle with icing sugar.

Preparation time: approx. 50 minutes
Per serving: approx. 293 kcal/1230 kj,
8 g P, 18 g L, 21 g G

Kiwi Fruit and Almond Cake

FOR 12 SERVINGS:

3 egg yolks

170 g/5$^{1}/_{2}$ oz sugar

1 tbsp vanilla sugar

125 g/4$^{1}/_{2}$ oz soft butter

A pinch of salt

150 g/5 oz plain flour

200 g/7 oz kiwi fruit

200 g/7 oz ground almonds

150 g/5 oz double cream

250 ml/9 fl oz Amaretto

Butter, to grease the baking tin

Kiwi fruit slices, to garnish

1. Mix the egg yolk with 70 g/ 2$^{1}/_{2}$ oz of the sugar and the vanilla sugar in a bowl. Add the butter and salt and then the flour, kneading into a dough. Roll into a ball, wrap in cling film and leave to stand in a cool place for 1 hour.

2. Peel the kiwi fruit and cut into slices. Stir together the almonds, remaining sugar and egg yolk, the double cream and Amaretto and place to one side.

3. Preheat the oven to 200 °C/ 390 °F/gas mark 6. Grease a 24 cm/9$^{1}/_{2}$ in springform baking tin with butter and dust with flour.

4. Roll out the short crust dough between two sheets of cling film, and line the baking tin with it, making sure that there is plenty overlapping.

5. Form a generous 3cm/1$^{1}/_{4}$ in high pastry rim using your fingers. Fill the base with kiwi slices, saving some for garnishing later. Pour in the almond mix and smooth off the top.

6. Place on the middle shelf of the oven and bake for 40 minutes. After approx. 20 minutes cover the top of the cake with aluminium foil, to prevent it from getting too dark.

7. When ready remove from the baking tin and place on a cake cooling rack. Garnish with the kiwi fruit slices before serving.

Preparation time: approx. 45 minutes (excluding standing time)
Per serving: approx. 444 kcal/1867 kj, 7 g P, 26 g L, 31 g G

Apricot Pie

FOR 12 SERVINGS:

250 g/9 oz plain wheat flour

130 g/4½ oz butter

1 tbsp milk

100 g/3½ oz sugar

2 egg yolks

A pinch of salt

Butter, to grease the baking tin

100 g/3½ oz finely crushed sponge fingers

600 g/1 lb 5 oz apricots

1 carambole (star fruit)

1 egg, to brush

Icing sugar, to decorate

1. Mix together the flour, sugar, butter, milk, salt, egg and knead into a smooth dough. Roll the dough into a ball, wrap in cling film and leave to stand in a cool place for approx. 1 hour.

2. Grease a 24 cm/9½ in spring-form baking tin with butter and sprinkle with the crushed sponge fingers. Trim, wash and dry the apricots, cut in half and remove the stones. Wash and dry the carambole and cut into slices. Preheat the oven to 225 °C/440 °F/ gas mark 7.

3. Roll the dough onto a flour-covered working surface and line the baking tin with it. Cover the base with the apricots, cut off the excess dough, pressing the edges against the tin. Roll the remaining dough out into a round lid.

4. Lay the lid over the fruit. Beat an egg and brush the surface, piercing the dough several times with a fork. Place on the middle shelf of the oven and bake for approx. 25 minutes. Sprinkle with icing sugar before serving.

Preparation time: approx. 50 minutes
Per serving: approx. 250 kcal/1050 kj,
4 g P, 12 g L, 29 g G

Step 3

Step 4

Mandarin Cake

FOR 12 SERVINGS:

200 g/7 oz plain wheat flour

A pinch of salt

60 g/2 oz sugar

100 g/3¹/₂ oz butter, chopped

1 kg/2 lbs 3 oz low fat quark

200 g/7 oz mandarins (preserved)

75 ml/2¹/₂ fl oz brown rum

Butter, to grease the baking tin

3 tbsp breadcrumbs

100 g/3¹/₂ oz apricot jam

4 tbsp lemon juice

100 g/3¹/₂ oz icing sugar

5 egg yolks

50 g/1³/₄ oz butter

3 egg whites

Cocoa powder, to decorate

1. Sift the flour onto a working surface. Add salt, sugar and butter pieces.

2. Chop up finely and then knead everything into a smooth dough while gradually adding 4 tablespoons ice cold water. Roll into a ball, wrap in cling film and leave to stand in a cool place for approx. 1 hour.

3. Completely drain the quark and mandarins. Warm the rum up gently in a saucepan and add the mandarin leaving them to draw for 2 minutes. Preheat the oven to 180 °C/355 °F/gas mark 4.

4. Grease a 24 cm/9¹/₂ in springform baking tin and dust with the breadcrumbs. Roll the dough out on a flour-covered working surface and line the baking tin with it. Spread the base with the jam.

5. Place the mandarins on top. Mix the quark with lemon juice, icing sugar, egg yolk and butter and stir well. Whisk the egg white until it is stiff and fold in carefully. Cover the mandarins with the quark mix and smooth it off. Place on the middle shelf of the oven and bake for approx. 50 minutes. When ready remove from tin and allow to cool. Before serving dust with cocoa powder.

Preparation time: approx. 1 hour
(excluding standing time)
Per serving: approx. 379 kcal/1592 kj,
10 g P, 24 g L, 25 g G

Fig Tart

FOR 12 SERVINGS:

3 eggs

100 g/3½ oz sugar

1 tbsp vanilla sugar

150 g/5 oz plain flour

A pinch of salt

100 g/3½ oz butter

Rind of ½ an untreated lemon

A pinch of cinnamon powder

A pinch of cardamom powder

A pinch of clove powder

3 tbsp custard powder

100 g/3½ oz ground cashew nuts

200 g/7 oz dried figs

Butter, to grease the baking tin

3 tbsp Arak (spirit)

Icing sugar, to decorate

2 fresh figs

2 tbsp whole cashew nuts

1. Whisk the eggs until foamy and light. Little by little add the sugar, vanilla sugar, flour and salt and whisk until the sugar completely dissolves. Fold in the butter. Preheat the oven to 200 °C/390 °F/ gas mark 6.

2. Stir in the lemon rind, spices, custard powder and cashew nuts. Wash the dried figs, dab dry and fold them into the mix.

3. Grease a 24 cm/9½ in spring-form baking tin. Spoon in the ready dough mix and place on the middle shelf of the oven and bake for approx. 35 minutes.

4. When ready, remove from the tin, dribble over the Arak and leave to cool.

5. Sprinkle with icing sugar, and garnish with the cashew nuts and fig slices before serving.

Preparation time: approx. 50 minutes
Per serving: approx. 330 kcal/1385 kj,
7 g P, 17 g L, 32 g G

Step 4

Fine Fruit Tart

FOR 12 SERVINGS:

300 g/10¹/₂ oz flaky pastry (frozen)

1 egg yolk

300 g/10¹/₂ oz cream cheese

2 tbsp sugar

1 tbsp vanilla sugar

¹/₂ tsp freshly grated ginger

2 tbsp ginger jam

3 leaves of white gelatine

2 bananas

2 mangoes

200 g/7 oz cape gooseberries (physalis)

1. Slice each portion of flaky pastry in two. Cut out a 1 cm/¹/₃ in wide rectangular frame out of each piece and put to one side. Preheat the oven to 200 °C/390 °F/ gas mark 6.

2. Roll out the remaining pieces until they fit exactly under the cut out frames. Take the pastry frames and brush with water, then press them onto the rolled out rectangles.

3. Take a baking tray, sprinkle with a little water and place the prepared pastry on it. Whisk the egg yolk and then brush it onto the pastry. Place on the middle shelf of the oven and bake for approx. 15 minutes. If the pastry has risen in the middle press down with a spoon.

4. Stir together the cream cheese, sugar, vanilla sugar, ginger and ginger jam. Soak the gelatine in a saucepan with some water, heat up until it dissolves, drain and stir into the cream mix.

5. Peel the bananas and cut into slices. Peel the mangoes and cut in half and then into thin strips. Peel the cape gooseberries.

6. Remove the flaky pastry from the oven, allow to cool, fill with the cream, garnish with the fruit pieces and serve.

Preparation time: approx. 45 minutes
Per serving: approx. 212 kcal/890 kj,
5 g P, 12 g L, 17 g G

Melon Cake

FOR 12 SERVINGS:

6 eggs

2 tbsp lukewarm water

370 g/13 oz sugar

A pinch of salt

90 g/3 oz butter

150 g/5 oz plain flour

A pinch of baking powder

Butter, to grease the baking tin

1 cantaloupe melon,
approx. 1 kg/2 lbs 3 oz

375 ml/13 fl oz white port wine

3 tbsp lemon juice

12 leaves of white gelatine

250 ml/9 fl oz whipping cream

1 tbsp vanilla sugar

1. Preheat the oven to 180 °C/ 355 °F/gas mark 4. Separate the eggs. Mix the egg yolks and water in a bowl and whisk until foamy and light. Add 175 g/6 oz of the sugar, salt and butter. Continue to whisk until thick and creamy. Whisk the egg white while adding 45 g/1¹/₂ oz of the sugar until it is stiff. Fold ¹/₃ of this into the egg yolk mix. Mix the flour and baking powder and sift over the egg yolk mix. Now fold in the remaining egg snow.

2. Grease a 24 cm/9¹/₂ in spring-form baking tin and turn the dough mix into it. Place on the middle shelf of the oven and bake for approx. 30 minutes. Place on a cake rack to cool.

3. Cut the melon in half and scrape the fruit out with a melon scoop. Place a cake ring around the sponge base and then fill the sponge with the melon balls.

4. Gently heat the port with 125 ml/4¹/₂ fl oz water, lemon juice and 150 g/5 oz of the sugar until the sugar has dissolved.

5. Soak the gelatine in some cold water, press dry and then add to the warm port wine to fully dissolve. Leave to cool a little. Whisk the cream until it is stiff and fluffy, sweeten with the vanilla sugar and fold into the port wine mix.

6. Shortly before the mixture gels spoon it over the melon balls, filling all gaps and then place in the fridge to completely cool. Remove the cake ring and cut the melon cake into slices.

Preparation time: approx. 50 minutes (excluding standing time)
Per serving: approx. 400 kcal/1678 kj, 6 g P, 15 g L, 48 g G

Step 5

Lychee Coconut Cake

FOR 12 SERVINGS:

125 g/4¹/₂ oz low fat quark

75 g/2¹/₂ oz sugar

1 egg

A pinch of salt

2 tbsp oil

3 tbsp milk

200 g/7 oz plain wheat flour

1 tsp baking powder

800 g/1 lb 12 oz lychees (tinned)

6 egg whites

300 g/10¹/₂ oz icing sugar

A pinch of ginger powder

A pinch of clove powder

300 g/10¹/₂ oz desiccated coconut

Butter, to grease the baking tray

Chopped mint, to garnish

1. Stir together the quark, sugar, egg, oil and milk. Mix together the flour and baking powder and sift over the quark mix, gradually kneading it in.

2. Roll the dough into a ball, wrap in cling film and leave to stand in a cool place for approx. 1 hour. Preheat the oven to 175 °C/350 °F/ gas mark 3–4.

3. Drain the lychees. Whisk the egg white until it is stiff and then sift over with the icing sugar folding it in gradually, while also adding the spices and desiccated coconut.

4. Grease a baking tray with butter, roll the dough out onto it and cut several small crosses into it.

5. Smooth the whisked egg mixture over the dough and then distribute the lychees on top. Place on the middle shelf of the oven and bake for approx. 35 minutes. Before serving garnish with the mint.

Preparation time: approx. 45 minutes
(excluding standing time)
Per serving: approx. 190 kcal/796 kj,
2,5 g P, 6,5 g L, 28 g G

Step 5

Exotic Meringue Baskets

FOR 4 BASKETS:

4 egg whites	
170 g/5½ oz sugar	
60 g/2 oz ground almonds	
20 g/¾ oz icing sugar	
½ tsp plain flour	
250 g/9 oz figs	
250 g/9 oz pineapple chunks (tinned)	
100 g/3½ oz whipping cream	
1 tsp Kirsch	
1 tbsp vanilla sugar	

1. Whisk the egg white until it is stiff and gradually sprinkle over the sugar. Carefully fold in the almonds, icing sugar and flour.

2. Preheat the oven to 160 °C/ 320 °F/gas mark 2–3. Cover a baking tray with greaseproof paper and mark 4 x 10 cm/4 in circles with a pen. Turn the marked side face downwards.

3. Fill an icing bag with the egg mix, attach a star shaped nozzle and squeeze out 4 rings along the markings on the greaseproof paper.

4. Use the rest of the cream mix to make creamy blobs filling the top of the ring. Place on the middle shelf of the oven and bake for approx. 35 minutes.

5. Turn the oven off, open the door and leave the meringues in there to cool.

6. Peel the figs and cut into wedges. Drain the pineapple. Place some of the fruit to one side for garnishing. Turn the figs and pineapple chunks into the meringue baskets.

7. Whisk the cream together with the vanilla sugar and Kirsch until it is stiff and then top the fruit with it. Garnish with the rest of the fruit and serve.

Preparation time: approx. 50 minutes
Per serving: approx. 434 kcal/1824 kj,
7 g P, 14 g L, 65 g G

Pineapple Crunch

FOR 8 SERVINGS:

300 g/10½ oz short crust pastry
(ready-made)

Sugar, for working surface

50 g/1¾ oz pineapple jam

1 pineapple

50 ml/1¾ fl oz Campari

50 g/1¾ oz sugar

100 g/3½ oz desiccated coconut

1. Roll the short crust pastry onto a sugar covered working surface and use to line two 12 cm/4¾ in pie dishes. Spread the pineapple jam over the dough.

2. Peel the pineapple, cut into slices and then cut the fruit flesh into small chunks. Preheat the oven to 180 °C/355 °F/gas mark 4.

3. Dribble the Campari and sugar over the pineapple pieces.

4. Turn the fruit into the lined moulds and sprinkle over with the desiccated coconut.

5. Place on the middle shelf of the oven and bake for approx. 25 minutes until golden brown.

Preparation time: approx. 50 minutes
Per serving: approx. 269 kcal/1131 kj,
4,5 g P, 7,5 g L, 40 g G

Mangosteen Tart

FOR 12 SERVINGS:

300 g/10½ oz short crust pastry (frozen)

Butter, to grease the dish

3 eggs

300 g/10½ oz ricotta

60 g/2 oz sugar

Juice and rind of 1 untreated lemon

300 g/10½ oz mangosteen (Malaysian berries)

300 g/10½ oz custard apples (cherimoya fruit)

1. Roll the pastry out onto a flour-covered working surface and use to line a 24 cm/9½ in greased pie dish.

2. Separate the eggs. Whisk the egg yolks with the cream cheese, sugar, lemon juice and lemon rind until foamy and light. Preheat the oven to 180 °C/355 °F/gas mark 4.

3. Whisk the egg white until it is stiff and fold into the egg yolk and then turn into the pastry lined dish. Wash the mangosteens, break open and remove the fruit segments. Peel the cherimoya and cut into small pieces. Distribute the fruit over the egg mix.

4. Place on the middle shelf of the oven and bake for approx. 40 minutes.

Preparation time: approx. 50 minutes
Per serving: approx. 196 kcal/824 kj,
7 g P, 6 g L, 24 g G

Step 1

Step 2

Kiwi Meringue Slices

FOR 24 SERVINGS:

300 g/10½ oz plain wheat flour

200 g/7 oz butter, chopped

70 g/2½ oz icing sugar

A pinch of salt

¼ tsp rind of 1 untreated lemon

1 egg

800 g/1 lb 12 oz kiwi fruit

4 egg whites

100 g/3½ oz sugar

200 g/7 oz hazelnut flakes

Icing sugar, to decorate

Fresh mint, to garnish

1. Add the flour, butter pieces, icing sugar, salt, lemon rind and egg to a working surface and chop up finely. Knead everything together and roll into a ball, wrap in cling film and leave to stand in a cool place for approx. 1 hour. Preheat the oven to 200 °C/390 °F/gas mark 6.

2. Peel the kiwi fruit and cut into slices. Roll the dough onto a greaseproof paper covered baking tray. Arrange the kiwi fruit slices on the dough and place on the middle shelf of the oven and bake for approx. 30 minutes.

3. While waiting whisk the egg white until it is stiff, while gradually adding the sugar. Remove the cake from the oven and brush with the meringue mix. Cover with the hazelnut flakes. Bake for a further 10 minutes at 180 °C/355 °F/gas mark 4. Sprinkle with icing sugar, garnish with the mint and serve.

Preparation time: approx. 50 minutes
(excluding standing time)
Per serving: approx. 215 kcal/906 kj,
3 g P, 12 g L, 19 g G

Step 1

Step 2

Pineapple Nut Cake

FOR 24 SERVINGS:

300 g/10½ oz rye flour
200 g/7 oz butter, chopped
170 g/5½ oz icing sugar
A pinch of salt
A pinch of lemon rind of 1 untreated lemon
1 egg
750 g/1 lb 11 oz pineapple rings (tinned)
50 g/1¾ oz sugar
100 g/3½ oz cashew nuts
4 tbsp lemon juice

1. Add the flour, butter, 70 g/ 2½ oz of the icing sugar, salt, lemon rind and egg to a working surface and chop up finely. Knead everything together, roll into a ball, wrap in cling film and leave to stand in a cool place for approx. 1 hour. Preheat the oven to 200 °C/ 390 °F/gas mark 6.

2. Drain the pineapple rings and cut in half. Sprinkle over with the sugar and leave briefly to draw.

3. Cover a greaseproof paper lined baking tray with the dough, and place the pineapple rings on it. Coarsely chop up the cashew nuts and sprinkle over the pineapple. Place on the middle shelf of the oven and bake for approx. 20 minutes.

4. Stir the rest of the icing sugar in with the lemon juice and brush over the cake when ready baked and then serve.

Preparation time: approx. 50 minutes
(excluding standing time)
Per serving: approx. 189 kcal/795 kj,
2 g P, 9 g L, 22 g G

Step 1

Step 2

109

Kumquat Pastries

FOR 6 PASTRIES:

250 g/9 oz flaky pastry

150 g/5 oz sugar

300 g/10^{1}/$_{2}$ oz kumquats

3 tbsp honey

8 tbsp port wine

3 tbsp cornflour

1. Roll the flaky pastry out onto a sugar covered working surface, and cut out into 12 circles. Lay on a greaseproof paper covered baking tray. Preheat the oven to 200 °C/390 °F/gas mark 6.

2. Wash and dry the kumquats and cut into slices. Add to a saucepan together with the port wine and honey and heat up gently for approx. 5 minutes. Towards the end thicken with the cornflour.

3. Spoon the fruit onto the centre of six of the dough circles, and then top with the other six circles pressing down on the edges to seal them. Place on the middle shelf of the oven and bake for 20 minutes.

Preparation time: approx. 45 minutes
Per serving: approx. 353 kcal/1485 kj,
2 g P, 13 g L, 52 g G

Physalis Cake

FOR 24 SERVINGS:

1160 ml/5^{1}/$_{2}$ fl oz milk

400 g/14 oz plain wheat flour

30 g/1 oz fresh yeast

260 g/9^{1}/$_{2}$ oz butter

40 g/1^{1}/$_{2}$ oz sugar

A pinch of salt

1 egg

2 egg yolks

500 g/1 lb 2 oz cape gooseberries (physalis)

100 g/3^{1}/$_{2}$ oz honey

150 g/5 oz plain wheat flour, for the crumble

100 g/3^{1}/$_{2}$ oz walnut kernels

1. Heat the milk in a saucepan. Sift the flour into a bowl, make a hollow in the middle and crumble the yeast into it. Pour the milk over it. Knead everything together and leave to rise in a warm place for approx. 20 minutes.

2. Knead 60 g/2 oz of the butter, sugar, salt, 1 egg and 1 egg yolk into the dough. Roll the dough into a ball, cover and leave to stand until it has doubled in size. Preheat the oven to 200 °C/390 °F/ gas mark 6.

3. Wash the cape gooseberries and cut in half. Stir the rest of the butter with the honey until foamy and then add the remaining egg yolks. Finally fold in the flour and

rub with the fingers until it becomes a crumbly dough.

4. Roll the yeast dough onto a flour-covered working surface and place on a greaseproof paper covered baking tray. Spread the cape gooseberries onto the dough and sprinkle over with the crumble. Top off with the walnut kernels. Place on the middle shelf of the oven and bake for approx. 40 minutes.

Preparation time: approx. 1 hour
(excluding standing time)
Per serving: approx. 200 kcal/842 kj,
4 g P, 10 g L, 20 g G

Step 4

"Tarte Tropicale"

FOR 24 SERVINGS:

300 g/10½ oz plain wheat flour

200 g/7 oz butter, chopped

70 g icing sugar

A pinch of salt

¼ tsp grated rind of 1 untreated lemon

1 egg

400 g/14 oz cream cheese

80 ml/2½ fl oz raspberry liqueur

2 carambola (star fruit)

1 small mango

3 kiwi fruits

3 tbsp lemon juice

1 tbsp vanilla sugar

1. Add the flour, butter pieces, icing sugar, salt, lemon rind and egg to a working surface and chop up finely. Knead everything together, roll into a ball, wrap in cling film and leave to stand in a cool place for approx. 1 hour. Preheat the oven to 200 °C/390 °F/ gas mark 6.

2. Roll the dough out onto a flour-covered working surface and then use it to line a 24 cm/9½ in pie dish. Place on the middle shelf of the oven and bake for approx. 15 minutes.

3. Stir the raspberry liqueur into the cream cheese. Wash and dry the fruit and cut it into slices and strips. Sprinkle over with the lemon juice and vanilla sugar.

4. Spoon the cream cheese onto the tart base and smooth off. Top with the fruit pieces and serve.

Preparation time: approx. 50 minutes
(excluding standing time)
Per serving: approx. 171 kcal/721 kj,
3 g P, 9 g L, 14 g G

Step 3

Pumpkin Mango Cake

FOR 24 SERVINGS:

160 ml/5¹/₂ fl oz milk

400 g/14 oz plain wheat flour

30 g/1 oz fresh yeast

60 g/2 oz butter

40 g/1¹/₂ oz sugar

A pinch of salt

1 egg

1 egg yolk

800 g/1 lb 12 oz pumpkin flesh

200 g/7 oz mango

400 g/14 oz brown sugar

100 ml/3¹/₂ fl oz Curacao blue

2 tbsp lemon juice

1 tsp ginger powder

A pinch of cardamom powder

Icing sugar, to decorate

1. Heat the milk in a saucepan. Sift the flour into a bowl, make a hollow in the middle and crumble the yeast into it. Pour the milk over it. Knead everything together and leave to rise in a warm place for approx. 20 minutes.

2. Knead the butter, sugar, salt, egg and egg yolk into the dough. Roll the dough into a ball, cover and leave to stand until it has doubled in size.

3. Preheat the oven to 200 °C/ 390 °F/gas mark 6. While waiting cut the pumpkin and peeled mango pieces into cubes and add to a saucepan with the rest of the ingredients. Heat up gently for approx. 20 minutes.

4. Roll the dough onto a grease-proof paper covered baking tray and then spoon on the pumpkin mango mix spreading it over the dough.

5. Place on the middle shelf of the oven and bake for approx. 25 minutes. Sprinkle with icing sugar before serving.

Preparation time: approx. 50 minutes (excluding standing time)
Per serving: approx. 182 kcal/767 kj, 3 g P, 4 g L, 30 g G

Fine Lychee Tartlets

FOR 8 TARTLETS:

300 g/10½ oz short crust pastry (ready-made)

200 g/7 oz marzipan paste

150 g/5 oz icing sugar

3 egg yolks

250 g/9 oz fresh lychees

200 g/7 oz mandarins (tinned)

2 tbsp ginger jam

Whipped cream, to decorate

1. Roll the short crust pastry out onto a flour-covered working surface and cut out into 8 cm/ 3¼ in circles. Place them on a greaseproof paper covered baking tray. Preheat the oven to 180 °C/ 355 °F/gas mark 4.

2. Stir the marzipan, icing sugar and egg yolk together until smooth and creamy. Fill into an icing bag with a star-shaped nozzle and squeeze out an edging on to the pastry circles.

3. Place on the middle shelf of the oven and bake for approx. 15 minutes.

4. Peel the lychees and drain the mandarins. Heat the jam in a saucepan and add the lychees and mandarin segments. Turn into the middle of the tartlet bases, top with a swirl of whipped cream and serve.

Preparation time: approx. 45 minutes
Per serving: approx. 437 kcal/1835 kj,
9 g P, 17 g L, 55 g G

Cherimoya Quark Cake

FOR 12 SERVINGS:

300 g/10¹/₂ oz short crust pastry
(ready-made)

Butter, to grease pie dish

2 eggs

75 g/2¹/₂ oz sugar

1 tbsp vanilla sugar

250 g/9 oz creme quark

6 tbsp cream

6 custard apples (cherimoyas)

50 g/1³/₄ oz chopped almonds

1. Roll out the short crust pastry onto flour-covered working surface, and line a 24 cm/9¹/₂ in, greased pie dish with it.

2. Whisk the egg with the sugar and vanilla sugar until foamy and light. Carefully fold in the quark and cream. Cut the cherimoyas in half and slice into small pieces removing the pips.

3. Spread the fruit onto the dough and spoon over the cream mix, smoothing it off.

4. Place on the middle shelf of the oven and bake for approx. 35 minutes.

Preparation time: approx. 40 minutes
Per serving: approx. 212 kcal/893 kj,
5 g P, 7 g L, 28 g G

Step 2

Oriental Fruit Cake

FOR 24 SERVINGS:

150 g/5 oz oat meal

150 g/5 oz plain coarse grained wheat flour

200 g/7 oz butter, chopped

70 g/2¹/₂ oz icing sugar

A pinch of salt

A pinch of grated rind of 1 untreated lemon

1 egg

350 g/12 oz figs

350 g/12 oz fresh dates

100 g/3¹/₂ oz crystallised ginger

200 g/7 oz plain wheat flour

100 g/3¹/₂ oz brown sugar

125 g/4¹/₂ oz margarine

50 g/1³/₄ oz sesame seeds

100 g/3¹/₂ oz chopped peanuts

1. Add the oatmeal, 150 g/5 oz flour, butter pieces, icing sugar, salt, lemon rind and the egg to a working surface and chop up finely. Knead everything together and roll into a ball, wrap in cling film and leave to stand in a cool place for approx. 1 hour. Preheat the oven to 200 °C/390 °F/gas mark 6.

2. Wash the figs and cut into wedges. Wash the dates, cut in half, remove the stones and chop into small pieces. Peel the ginger and chop into small pieces as well.

3. Roll the dough out onto a greaseproof paper covered baking tray and spread the fruit onto it.

4. Mix the sugar with 200 g/7 oz flour, and margarine and chop up finely. Rub and knead the mixture until it becomes crumbly. Sprinkle the finished crumble over the fruit, together with the sesame seeds and the chopped peanuts.

5. Place on the middle shelf of the oven and bake for approx. 30 minutes.

Preparation time: approx. 50 minutes
(excluding standing time)
Per serving: approx. 294 kcal/1236 kj,
4 g P, 13 g L, 35 g G

Yoghurt Mandarin Cake

FOR 24 SERVINGS:

300 g/10½ oz quark

8 tbsp oil

2 eggs

100 g/3½ oz sugar

400 g/14 oz plain wheat flour

½ tsp baking powder

4 tbsp milk

800 g/1 lb 12 oz mandarin (tinned)

5 egg yolk

1 tbsp cornflour

7 tbsp yoghurt

1 tsp grated rind of 1 untreated lemon

5 egg whites

1. Drain the quark in a sieve, pressing gently to rid any excess liquid.

2. Mix the quark together with the oil, eggs, flour, baking powder and milk and knead into a smooth dough. Preheat the oven to 180 °C/ 355 °F/gas mark 4.

3. Cover a baking try with grease-proof paper. Roll the dough onto a flour-covered working surface and then lay on the baking tray. Drain the mandarins. Place a bowl in a hot water jacket and then add the yoghurt, egg yolk and cornflour whisking until foamy and light. Add the lemon rind.

4. Whisk the egg white until it is stiff and then fold it together with the mandarins into the yoghurt mix. Spoon everything over the dough covering it completely. Place on the middle shelf of the oven and bake for approx. 30 minutes.

Preparation time: approx. 50 minutes
Per serving: approx. 181 kcal/763 kj,
5 g P, 8 g L, 18 g G

Step 3

Crunchy Treats Packed with Spices, Nuts, and Almonds

Cakes with an enticing aroma and bite

Winter Cake

FOR 12 SERVINGS:

150 g/5 oz butter

65 g/2 oz sultanas

65 g/2 oz candied orange peel

250 g/9 oz plain wheat flour

A pinch of salt

1 tsp baking powder

150 g/5 oz sugar

150 g/5 oz coarsely chopped pecan nuts

1 tbsp mulled wine

$^1/_2$ tsp clove powder

$^1/_2$ tsp cinnamon powder

125 g/4$^1/_2$ oz pear purée

125 g/4$^1/_2$ oz apple purée

Icing sugar, to decorate

1. Melt the butter slowly in a saucepan. Mix the sultanas, orange peel, flour, salt, sugar and baking powder together in a bowl. Preheat the oven to 175 °C/350 °F/gas mark 3–4.

2. Add the pecan nuts, mulled wine, spices, purée and the slightly cooled butter to the bowl and mix in. Knead everything together into a dough.

3. Spoon the mix into a 30 cm/ 12 in long loaf tin and smooth off. Place on the middle shelf of the oven and bake for approx. 1 hour. If the top of the cake starts to get too dark then cover with grease-proof paper or aluminium foil.

4. Remove the cake from the oven and leave to cool. Turn out of tin, sprinkle with icing sugar and serve on a plate.

Preparation time: approx. 1$^1/_2$ hour
Per serving: approx. 356 kcal/1498 kj,
3 g P, 19 g L, 38 g G

Step 2

Step 3

Winter Apple Cake

FOR 24 SERVINGS:

300 g/10½ oz plain wheat flour
200 g/7 oz butter, chopped
100 g/3½ oz sugar
A pinch of salt
A pinch of grated rind of
1 untreated lemon
1 egg
1 tsp gingerbread spices
500 g/1 lb 2 oz apples
3 tbsp lemon juice
25 g/1 oz chocolate, chopped
25 g/1 oz currants
50 g/1¾ oz ground almonds
1 tbsp rum
4 tbsp orange juice
100 g/3½ oz marzipan paste
50 g/1¾ oz icing sugar
200 g/7 oz chocolate coating
Icing sugar, to decorate

1. Add the flour, butter pieces, sugar, salt, lemon rind, egg and gingerbread spices to a working surface and chop up finely. Knead everything together and roll the resulting dough into a ball, wrap in cling film and leave to stand in a cool place for approx. 1 hour. Preheat the oven to 200 °C/390 °F/gas mark 6.

2. Wash and peel the apples cut them in half and remove the cores. Then cut into wedges and finally cubes, sprinkle with lemon juice and fold into the dough together with the currants, almonds and rum.

3. Roll the dough onto a grease-proof paper covered baking tray and then place on the middle shelf of the oven and bake for approx. 25 minutes.

4. Knead the orange juice, marzipan paste and icing sugar into a dough. Roll out onto a lightly flour-covered working surface and cut out star shapes.

5. Melt the chocolate coating in a bowl with a hot water jacket and decorate the cake with chocolate strips. Garnish with the marzipan stars and sprinkle with icing sugar.

Preparation time: approx. 50 minutes
(excluding standing time)
Per serving: approx. 212 kcal/890 kj,
3 g P, 9 g L, 14 g G

Julias Crunchy Cake

FOR 24 SERVINGS:

285 ml/^{1}/$_2$ pint milk

500 g/1 lb 2 oz wholemeal wheat flour

30 g/1 oz fresh yeast

110 g/4 oz butter

120 g/5 oz sugar

A pinch of salt

1 egg

1 egg yolk

150 g/5 oz hazelnut flakes

100 g/3^1/$_2$ oz brown sugar

125 g/4^1/$_2$ oz margarine

1 tsp cinnamon powder

100 g/3^1/$_2$ oz icing sugar

1. Heat gently 160 ml/5^1/$_2$ fl oz of the milk in a saucepan. Sift 400 g/ 14 oz of the flour into a bowl, make a hollow in the middle and crumble the yeast into it. Pour the milk over it. Knead everything together and leave to rise in a warm place for approx. 20 minutes.

2. Knead 60 g/2 oz of the butter, 40 g/1^1/$_2$ oz of the sugar, salt, egg and egg yolk into the dough. Roll the dough into a ball, cover and leave to stand until it has doubled in size.

3. Heat the rest of the milk in a saucepan with the rest of the butter. Bring to the boil and stir in the hazelnut flakes and the rest of the sugar and leave to cook for approx. 5 minutes.

4. Preheat the oven to 200 °C/ 390 °F/gas mark 6. Roll out the dough on a greaseproof paper covered baking tray and brush over with the hazelnut mix.

5. Mix together the remaining wholemeal flour with the brown sugar, margarine and brown sugar and rub into a crumble. Sprinkle over the dough and leave to rise a further 10 minutes.

6. Place on the middle shelf of the oven and bake for approx. 35 minutes.

7. While waiting stir 3 tablespoons water into the icing sugar and heat in a saucepan. Brush icing over the ready cake before serving.

Preparation time: approx. 50 minutes
(excluding standing time)
Per serving: approx. 216 kcal/910 kj,
4 g P, 9 g L, 27 g G

Spice Cake

FOR 24 SERVINGS:

60 g/2 oz candied lemon peel

60 g/2 oz candied orange peel

60 g/2 oz raisins

5 tbsp Armagnac (brandy)

150 g/5 oz plain wheat flour

150 g/5 oz wholemeal spelt flour

200 g/7 oz butter, chopped

170 g/5$^{1}/_{2}$ oz icing sugar

A pinch of salt

$^{1}/_{4}$ tsp grated rind of 1 untreated lemon

1 egg

1 tsp mace

1 tsp cardamom powder

1 tsp pimento powder

2 tsp cinnamon powder

100 g/3$^{1}/_{2}$ oz maple syrup

4 tbsp cognac

1. Coarsely chop up the candied lemon and orange peel and raisins. Place in a saucepan and gently heat with the Armagnac and leave to draw for 15 minutes.

2. Put the flour, butter pieces, 70 g/2$^{1}/_{2}$ oz of the icing sugar, salt, lemon rind and the egg to a bowl and mix well.

3. Add the spices and Armagnac fruit mix and knead everything together. Roll into a ball, wrap in cling film and leave to stand in a cool place for approx. 1 hour. Preheat the oven to 200 °C/390 °F/ gas mark 6.

4. Roll the dough out onto a greaseproof paper covered baking tray. Place on the middle shelf of the oven and bake for approx. 30 minutes.

5. Heat up the maple syrup with the cognac and stir in the remaining icing sugar. Remove the cake from the oven and brush with the syrup.

Preparation time: approx. 50 minutes (excluding standing time)
Per serving: approx. 171 kcal/720 kj, 2 g P, 8 g L, 23 g G

Step 2

Step 3

Rice Walnut Cake

FOR 24 SERVINGS:

300 g/10½ oz quark

8 tbsp oil

2 eggs

100 g/3½ oz sugar

400 g/14 oz plain wheat flour

½ tsp baking powder

400 ml/14 fl oz milk

150 g/5 oz rice

A few drops vanilla extract

2 tbsp margarine

2 egg yolks

3 tbsp vanilla sugar

100 g/3½ oz chopped walnuts

3 egg whites

Icing sugar, to decorate

1. Drain the quark through a sieve, pressing lightly to rid excess liquid.

2. Mix with the oil, eggs, sugar, flour, baking powder and 4 tablespoons of the milk and knead everything into a smooth dough.

3. Roll the dough out flat on greaseproof paper covered baking tray.

4. Add the rice to the remaining milk in a saucepan bring to the boil and add the vanilla sugar. Simmer gently for approx. 15 minutes and then leave to cool. Preheat the oven to 180 °C/ 355 °F/gas mark 4.

5. Mix the margarine with the egg yolk and the vanilla sugar and whisk until foamy and light. Add the walnuts.

6. Whisk the egg white until it is stiff. Add the egg yolk mix to the rice and then fold in the egg snow. Pour over the dough, smooth it over and then place on the middle shelf of the oven and bake for approx. 40 minutes. Sprinkle with icing sugar before serving.

Preparation time: approx. 50 minutes
Per serving: approx. 195 kcal/819 kj,
3 g P, 9 g L, 18 g G

Cappuccino Cake

FOR 24 SERVINGS:

300 g/10¹/₂ oz quark

50 g/3¹/₂ oz cocoa powder

8 tbsp oil

2 eggs

150 g/5 oz sugar

400 g/14 oz plain wheat flour

4 tsp baking powder

4 tbsp milk

2 cl/¹/₂ tsp Amaretto

4 tbsp cappuccino powder

100 g/3¹/₂ oz ground almonds

Butter, to grease the baking tin

White icing, to decorate

Almonds, to garnish

1. Drain the quark through a sieve, pressing lightly to rid excess liquid.

2. Mix with the oil, eggs, sugar, flour, baking powder and 4 table-spoons of the milk and knead everything into a smooth dough. Preheat the oven to 180 °C/355 °F/ gas mark 4.

3. Stir together the Amaretto with the cappuccino powder and ground almonds. Fold the resulting mix into the quark dough.

4. Grease a 24 cm/9¹/₂ in spring-form baking tin and fill with the dough smoothing off the top. Place on the middle shelf of the oven and bake for 25 minutes.

Decorate with the white icing and garnish with the almonds and then serve.

Preparation time: approx. 50 minutes
Per serving: approx. 147 kcal/621 kj,
3 g P, 7 g L, 19 g G

Step 3

125

Crumbly Poppy Cake

FOR 24 SERVINGS:

410 ml/14¹/₂ fl oz milk

200 g/7 oz wholemeal wheat flour

200 g/7 oz buckwheat flour

30 g/1 oz fresh yeast

90 g/3 oz butter

190 g/6¹/₂ oz sugar

A pinch of salt

1 egg

1 egg yolk

500 g/1 lb 2 oz ground poppy seeds

Grated rind of ¹/₂ an untreated lemon

100 g/3¹/₂ oz raisins

1 cl/shot of Korn (German spirit or use rye whisky)

200 g/7 oz plain wheat flour

100 g/3¹/₂ oz brown sugar

125 g/4¹/₂ oz margarine

100 g/3¹/₂ oz chopped almonds

1. Heat 160 ml/5¹/₂ fl oz of the milk in a saucepan. Sift the wholemeal and buckwheat flour into a bowl, make a hollow in the middle and crumble the yeast into it. Pour the milk over it. Knead everything together and leave to rise in a warm place for approx. 20 minutes.

2. Knead 60 g/2 oz of the butter, 40 g/1¹/₂ oz of the sugar, salt, egg and 1 egg yolk into the dough. Roll the dough into a ball, cover and leave to stand until it has doubled in size. Preheat the oven to 200 °C/390 °F/gas mark 6.

3. Roll out the dough onto a greaseproof paper covered baking tray.

4. Heat up the remaining milk in a saucepan adding the poppy and the remaining sugar and butter. Stir in the raisins and Korn (or rye whisky). Leave to cool and then brush onto the dough.

5. Mix together in a bowl the plain wheat flour with the brown sugar, margarine and almonds and then rub into a crumbly dough. Sprinkle the crumble over the poppy mix and then place on the middle shelf of the oven and bake for approx. 30 minutes.

Preparation time: approx. 50 minutes (excluding standing time)
Per serving: approx. 370 kcal/1554 kj, 8 g P, 19 g L, 35 g G

Chocolate Flapjack

FOR 24 SERVINGS:

660 ml/1 pint 3 fl oz milk

400 g/14 oz wholemeal wheat flour

30 g/1 oz fresh yeast

60 g/2 oz butter

140 g/4³/₄ oz sugar

A pinch of salt

1 egg

4 egg yolks

A few drops of vanilla extract

60 g/2 oz cocoa powder

30 g/1 oz flour

200 g/7 oz hazelnut flakes

1. Heat 160 ml/5^{1}/$_{2}$ fl oz of the milk in a saucepan. Sift the flour into a bowl, make a hollow in the middle and crumble the yeast into it. Pour the milk over it. Knead everything together and leave to rise in a warm place for approx. 20 minutes.

2. Knead the butter, 40 g/1^{1}/$_{2}$ oz of the sugar, salt, egg and 1 egg yolk into the dough. Roll the dough into a ball, cover and leave to stand until it has doubled in size. Preheat the oven to 200 °C/ 390 °F/gas mark 6.

3. Roll out the dough onto a greaseproof paper covered baking tray. Place on the middle shelf of the oven and bake for approx. 30 minutes. Remove from oven and leave to cool.

4. Heat up the remaining milk with vanilla extract and cocoa powder and bring to the boil. Whisk the remaining sugar and egg yolks until creamy adding the flour slowly. Stir into the boiling milk, reduce heat and leave to simmer for approx. 5 minutes, then leave to cool.

5. Spoon the chocolate cream onto the cake base, sprinkle with the hazelnut flakes and serve.

Preparation time: approx. 45 minutes (excluding standing time)
Per serving: approx. 208 kcal/874 kj, 5 g P, 10 g L, 20 g G

Step 4

Spelt Lemon Bread

For 24 servings:

160 ml/5¹/₂ fl oz milk

400 g/14 oz spelt flour

30 g/1 oz fresh yeast

110 g/4 oz butter

120 g/5 oz sugar

A pinch of salt

1 egg

1 egg yolk

100 g/3¹/₂ oz candied lemon peel

50 g/1³/₄ oz raisins

80 g/2³/₄ oz cashew nuts

Grated rind of 2 untreated lemons

Decorating sugar, to garnish

1. Heat the milk in a saucepan. Sift the spelt flour into a bowl, make a hollow in the middle and

crumble the yeast into it. Pour the milk over it. Knead everything together and leave to rise in a warm place for 20 minutes. Pre-heat the oven to 200 °C/390 °F/ gas mark 6.

2. Knead 60 g/2 oz of the butter, 40 g/1¹/₂ oz of the sugar, salt, egg and egg yolk, candied lemon peel, raisins and nuts into the dough. Roll the dough into a ball, cover and leave to stand until it has doubled in size.

3. Knead the lemon peel into the dough, and roll out into a small loaf form on a working surface. Place on a greaseproof paper covered baking tray.

4. Place the spelt lemon bread on the middle shelf of the oven and bake for approx. 20 minutes. Sprinkle with the decorating sugar.

Preparation time: approx. 50 minutes (excluding standing time)
Per serving: approx. 151 kcal/638 kj, 3 g P, 6 g L, 18 g G

Step 1

Crispy Nut Cake

FOR 24 SERVINGS:

160 ml/5½ fl oz milk

400 g/14 oz plain wheat flour

30 g/1 oz fresh yeast

160 g/5½ oz butter

40 g/1½ oz sugar

A pinch of salt

1 egg

1 egg yolk

250 g/9 oz pecan nuts

250 g/9 oz raisins

250 g/9 oz brown sugar

250 ml/9 fl oz whipping cream

250 g/9 oz coarsely chopped peanuts

6 tbsp whisky

1. Heat the milk in a saucepan. Sift the flour into a bowl, make a hollow in the middle and crumble the yeast into it. Pour the milk over it. Knead everything together and leave to rise in a warm place for approx. 20 minutes.

2. Knead 60 g/2 oz of the butter, 40 g/1½ oz of the sugar, salt, egg and egg yolk into the dough. Roll the dough into a ball, cover and leave to stand until it has doubled in size.

3. Preheat the oven to 200 °C/ 390 °F/gas mark 6. Chop the pecan nuts and raisins coarsely. Melt the butter in a saucepan

adding the brown sugar. Stir in the cream and bring briefly to the boil. Then add the chopped peanuts, pecans and raisins and then the whisky stirring continuously.

4. Roll the dough out onto a greaseproof paper covered baking tray.

5. Spoon the nut mix onto the dough and place on the middle shelf of the oven and bake for approx. 30 minutes.

Preparation time: approx. 50 minutes (excluding standing time)
Per serving: approx. 320 kcal/1345 kj, 6 g P, 21 g L, 22 g G

Crunchy Butter Cake

FOR 24 SERVINGS:

160 ml/5¹/₂ fl oz milk

400 g/14 oz wholemeal plain wheat flour

30 g/1 oz fresh yeast

260 g/9¹/₂ oz butter

100 g/3¹/₂ oz sugar

A pinch of salt

1 egg

1 egg yolk

3 tbsp margarine

200 g/7 oz rolled oats

A pinch of aniseed powder

¹/₂ tsp ground coriander

1 tsp cinnamon powder

1. Heat the milk in a saucepan. Sift the flour into a bowl, make a hollow in the middle and crumble the yeast into it. Pour the milk over it. Knead everything together and leave to rise in a warm place for approx. 20 minutes.

2. Knead 60 g/2 oz of the butter, 40 g/1¹/₂ oz of the sugar, salt, egg and egg yolk into the dough. Roll the dough into a ball, cover and leave to stand until it has doubled in size.

3. Preheat the oven to 200 °C/ 390 °F/gas mark 6. Melt the margarine in a saucepan add the rolled oats and lightly roast. Sprinkle over the aniseed powder and ground coriander and stir in.

4. Roll the dough out onto a greaseproof paper covered baking tray. Spread the rest of the butter onto the dough and then sprinkle with the remaining sugar and the cinnamon powder. Lastly top everything off by sprinkling with the rolled oats. Place on the middle shelf of the oven and bake for approx. 30 minutes.

Preparation time: approx. 45 minutes
(excluding standing time)
Per serving: approx. 201 kcal/845 kj,
3 g P, 10 g L, 20 g G

Preparation time: approx. 1¹/₂ hour
Per serving: approx. 158 kcal/664 kj,
3 g P, 9 g L, 12 g G

Westphalian Bread Cake

FOR 24 SERVINGS:

150 g/5 oz dark rye bread
(or pumpernickel)

6 eggs

130 g/4½ oz icing sugar

70 g/2½ oz grated chocolate

100 g/3½ oz ground hazelnuts

2 tsp cinnamon powder

½ tsp clove powder

A pinch of aniseed powder

Grated rind of 1 untreated lemon

125 ml/4½ fl oz sherry

125 ml/4½ fl oz red wine

400 g/14 oz whipping cream

8 tbsp sea buckthorn jelly

4 tbsp chocolate flakes

1. Preheat the oven to 180 °C/ 355 °F/gas mark 4. Place the rye bread on the middle shelf of the oven and allow to dry for 8 minutes.

2. Separate the eggs. Whisk the egg yolk with the icing sugar until it is foamy and light. Add to it the grated chocolate, hazelnuts, cinnamon, clove and aniseed powders and the lemon rind and stir well.

3. Whisk the egg white until it is stiff and carefully fold into the egg spice mix.

4. Remove the rye bread from the oven and finely grate it into a bowl with the sherry and red wine and stir well. Fold into the dough.

5. Spoon the mixture onto a greaseproof paper covered baking tray, smoothing it down. Place on the middle shelf of the oven and bake for approx. 60 minutes.

6. While waiting whisk the cream until light and fluffy, adding the buckthorn jelly. Spread onto the baked bread cake and serve with a sprinkling of the chocolate flakes.

Step 2

Step 3

131

Canadian Nut Tart

FOR 24 SERVINGS:

300 g/10¹/₂ oz plain wheat flour

200 g/7 oz butter, chopped

70 g/2¹/₂ oz icing sugar

A pinch of salt

¹/₄ tsp grated rind of 1 untreated lemon

3 eggs

2 tbsp double cream

200 g/7 oz maple syrup

200 g/7 oz chopped pecan nuts

Butter, to grease the pie dish

Chopped pecan nuts, to garnish

Decorating sugar

1. Add the flour, butter pieces, icing sugar, salt, lemon rind, and egg to a working surface and chop up finely. Knead everything together and roll the resulting dough into a ball, wrap in cling film and leave to stand in a cool place for approx. 1 hour. Preheat the oven to 200 °C/390 °F/gas mark 6.

2. Stir together the remaining eggs in a bowl with the double cream, syrup and chopped pecan nuts.

3. Roll the dough onto a flour-covered working surface and place in a margarine lined 24 cm/9¹/₂ in pie dish. Pour over with the syrup mix and spread thinly. Place on the middle shelf of the oven and bake for approx. 35 minutes. Before serving sprinkle with the pecan nuts and decorating sugar.

Preparation time: approx. 50 minutes
(excluding standing time)
Per serving: approx. 217 kcal/912 kj,
2 g P, 13 g L, 18 g G

Step 1

Step 2

132

Students Pastry

FOR 24 SERVINGS:

300 g/10½ oz rye flour

200 g/7 oz butter, chopped

70 g/2½ oz icing sugar

A pinch of salt

A pinch of grated rind of 1 untreated lemon

1 egg

300 g/10½ oz mixed nuts and raisins

200 g/7 oz cream cheese

A pinch of pimento powder

A pinch of aniseed powder

Icing sugar, to garnish

Redcurrants, to garnish

1. Add the flour, butter pieces, icing sugar, salt, lemon rind, and egg to a working surface and chop up finely. Knead everything together and roll the resulting dough into a ball, wrap in cling film and leave to stand in a cool place for approx. 1 hour. Preheat the oven to 200 °C/390 °F/gas mark 6.

2. Mix together the mixed nuts and raisins with the cream cheese and spices.

3. Roll the dough out onto a flour-covered working surface and then line a 24 cm/9½ in springform baking tin with it. Place on the middle shelf of the oven and bake for approx. 15 minutes.

4. Spread the cheese and nut mix onto the dough and bake for about a further 15 minutes again on the middle shelf. Sprinkle with icing sugar, garnish with redcurrants and serve.

Preparation time: approx. 50 minutes (excluding standing time)
Per serving: approx. 217 kcal/913 kj, 5 g P, 14 g L, 13 g G

Step 1

Step 2

Almond Tartlets

FOR 12 TARTLETS:

300 g/10½ oz sweet peeled almonds

2 cl/½ tsp almond liqueur

100 g/3½ oz sultanas

200 g/7 oz margarine

150 g/5 oz sugar

4 eggs

240 g/8½ oz flour

80 g/2¾ oz cream cheese

Butter, to grease the small tartlet moulds

Icing sugar, to decorate

1. Leave the almonds to soak in the almond liqueur for approx. 15 minutes, and drain when ready.

2. Stir the sultanas together with the almonds, margarine, sugar and eggs in a mixing bowl. Preheat the oven to 180 °C/355 °F/gas mark 4.

3. Sift the flour into the bowl and knead into the mix together with the cream cheese. Grease the small moulds with butter and fill each with the dough. Place on the middle shelf of the oven and bake for approx. 30 minutes. Sprinkle with icing sugar before serving.

Preparation time: approx. 50 minutes
Per serving: approx. 192 kcal/809 kj,
4 g P, 14 g L, 10 g G

Sweet Plaited Loaf

FOR 24 SERVINGS:

160 ml/5½ fl oz milk

300 g/10½ oz plain wheat flour

50 g/1¾ oz ground peanuts

100 g/3½ oz ground pecan nuts

30 g/1 oz fresh yeast

60 g/2 oz butter

40 g/1½ oz brown sugar

A pinch of salt

1 egg

1 egg yolk

2 tbsp nut liqueur

2 tbsp truffle butter

Sesame and poppy seeds, to garnish

1. Heat the milk in a saucepan. Sift the flour into a bowl and add the ground peanuts and pecan nuts, make a hollow in the middle and crumble the yeast into it. Pour the milk over it. Knead everything together and leave to rise in a warm place for approx. 20 minutes.

2. Knead the butter, sugar, salt, egg and egg yolk and nut liqueur into the dough. Roll the dough into a ball, cover and leave to stand until it has doubled in size. Preheat the oven to 200 °C/390 °F/ gas mark 6.

3. Roll the dough out onto a flour-covered working surface and separate into three lengths. Plait

together into a loaf. Place the plaited loaf on a greaseproof paper covered baking tray. Brush with the truffle butter and then sprinkle with the poppy and sesame seeds. Place on the middle shelf of the oven and bake for approx. 30 minutes.

Preparation time: approx. 50 minutes (excluding standing time)
Per serving: approx. 111 kcal/469 kj, 2 g P, 5 g L, 10 g G

Step 3

Nutty Bread Ring

FOR 24 SERVINGS:

160 ml/5¹/₂ fl oz milk

400 g/14 oz plain wheat flour

30 g/1 oz fresh yeast

60 g/2 oz butter

40 g/1¹/₂ oz sugar

A pinch of salt

1 egg

1 egg yolk

2 cl/¹/₂ tsp Arak (spirit)

120 g/5 oz linseed

1 tsp turmeric

120 g/5 oz chopped pecan nuts

100 g/3¹/₂ oz grated carrots

100 g/3¹/₂ oz chopped almonds

100 g/3¹/₂ oz chopped walnuts

1. Heat the milk in a saucepan. Sift the flour into a bowl, make a hollow in the middle and crumble the yeast into it. Pour the milk over it. Knead everything together and leave to rise in a warm place for approx. 20 minutes.

2. Knead the butter, sugar, salt, egg and egg yolk into the dough. Roll the dough into a ball, cover and leave to stand until it has doubled in size.

3. Preheat the oven to 200 °C/ 390 °F/gas mark 6. Separate the dough into 4 equal portions. Knead the Arak and linseed into one portion. Then take a second portion and knead the turmeric and chopped pecan nuts into it.

Knead the chopped almonds and grated carrots into the third portion and the chopped walnuts into the fourth. Leave all the portions to rise for a further 10 minutes.

4. Roll out each dough portion onto a flour-covered working surface and break off and into small bread roll sized pieces. Press the rolls next to each other in a spiral pattern starting from the middle on a greaseproof paper covered baking tray. Place on the middle shelf of the oven and bake for approx. 25 minutes.

Preparation time: approx. 45 minutes (excluding standing time)
Per serving: approx. 212 kcal/891 kj, 5 g P, 13 g L, 15 g G

St Martins Bread

FOR 24 SERVINGS:

160 ml/5½ fl oz milk

400 g/14 oz plain wheat flour

30 g/1 oz fresh yeast

60 g/2 oz butter

40 g/1½ oz sugar

A pinch of salt

1 egg

2 egg yolk

200 g/7 oz banana chips

120 ml/4¼ fl oz grape juice

80 g/2¾ oz chopped hazelnuts

40 g/1½ oz candied orange peel

1 tsp gingerbread spices

2 tbsp split cardamom seeds

1. Heat the milk in a saucepan. Sift the flour into a bowl, make a hollow in the middle and crumble the yeast into it. Pour the milk over it. Knead everything together and leave to rise in a warm place for approx. 20 minutes.

2. Knead the butter, sugar, salt, egg and egg yolk into the dough. Roll the dough into a ball, cover and leave to stand until it has doubled in size.

3. Put the banana chips in a bowl with the grape juice and leave to soak for approx. 10 minutes and then drain.

4. Add the chopped hazelnuts, candied orange peel, gingerbread spices and the cardamom capsules. Preheat the oven to 200 °C/ 390 °F/gas mark 6.

5. Roll the dough out onto a flour-covered working surface into a rectangle measuring approx. 25 x 30 cm/10 x 12 in. Place on a greaseproof paper covered baking tray. Spoon the banana mix onto the middle of the dough. Cut strips diagonally from the edge of the mixture outwards. Starting at one end take a strip and pull it over the mix, from one side and then the other, alternating along the length of the loaf, pressing each end down. Brush with the remaining egg yolk. Place on the middle shelf of the oven and bake for approx. 25 minutes.

Preparation time: approx. 45 minutes (excluding standing time)
Per serving: approx. 133 kcal/561 kj, 3 g P, 4 g L, 19 g G

Savoury Snacks Fresh out of the Oven

A treat for anybody who likes it wholesome and spicy

Oriental Mincemeat Flan

FOR 24 SERVINGS:

160 ml/5½ fl oz milk

400 g/14 oz plain wheat flour

30 g/1 oz fresh yeast

60 g/2 oz butter

1 tsp sugar

A pinch of salt

2 eggs

1 egg yolk

1 Spanish onion

150 g/5 oz fresh dates

2 tbsp pine nuts

600 g/1 lb 5 oz beef mincemeat

Salt

Freshly ground pepper

A pinch of cumin powder

Paprika powder

400 g/14 oz tomatoes

¼ bunch of coriander

150 g/5 oz grated goats cheese

1. Heat the milk in a saucepan. Sift the flour into a bowl, make a hollow in the middle and crumble the yeast into it. Pour the milk over it. Knead everything together and leave to rise in a warm place for approx. 20 minutes.

2. Knead the butter, sugar, salt, egg and egg yolk into the dough. Roll the dough into a ball, cover and leave to stand until it has doubled in size.

3. Peel the onions and chop into cubes. Wash the dates, remove the stones and chop up finely. Coarsely chop up the pine nuts.

4. Mix the chopped ingredients in a bowl with the mincemeat, remaining egg, salt, pepper, cumin and paprika powder.

5. Preheat the oven to 200 °C/ 390 °F/gas mark 6. Trim and wash the tomatoes and then cut them into slices. Roll the dough out onto a flour-covered working surface and then place on a baking tray.

6. Spread the meat mix onto the dough. Cover with the tomatoes. Wash and dry the coriander, pick off the leaves and spread over the tomatoes together with the cheese. Place on the middle shelf of the oven and bake for approx. 30 minutes.

Preparation time: approx. 45 minutes
(excluding standing time)
Per serving: approx. 187 kcal/788 kj,
9 g P, 8 g L, 16 g G

140

Multicoloured Party Pizza

FOR 24 SERVINGS:

160 ml/5$^{1}/_{2}$ fl oz milk

400 g/14 oz plain wheat flour

30 g/1 oz fresh yeast

60 g/2 oz butter

1 tsp sugar

A pinch of salt

1 egg

1 egg yolk

2 green bell peppers

2 red bell peppers

2 yellow bell peppers

200 g/7 oz tomatoes

150 g/5 oz Spanish onions

200 g/7 oz mushrooms

100 g/3$^{1}/_{2}$ oz Parma ham

4 tbsp ketchup

100 g/3$^{1}/_{2}$ oz tomato purée

$^{1}/_{2}$ bunch mixed herbs

100 g/3$^{1}/_{2}$ oz Gouda cheese

100 g/3$^{1}/_{2}$ oz mozarella

Basil cut into strips, to garnish

1. Heat the milk in a saucepan. Sift the flour into a bowl, make a hollow in the middle and crumble the yeast into it. Pour the milk over it. Knead everything together and leave to rise in a warm place for approx. 20 minutes.

2. Knead the butter, sugar, salt, egg and egg yolk into the dough. Roll the dough into a ball, cover and leave to stand until it has doubled in size.

3. Trim and wash the peppers and cut into strips. Trim and wash the tomatoes and cut into small wedges. Peel the onions and cut into rings. Trim and wash the mushrooms and cut into slices. Cut the ham into thin strips. Preheat the oven to 200 °C/390 °F/ gas mark 6.

4. Cover a baking tray with greaseproof paper and roll the dough onto it. Stir the ketchup together with the tomato purée and brush onto the dough. Spread the prepared vegetables over the tomato mix. Wash and dry the herbs, then chop up finely and sprinkle over the pizza.

5. Grate the Gouda cheese and cut the mozzarella into slices. Top off the pizza with the cheese. Place on the middle shelf of the oven and bake for approx. 25 minutes. Before serving garnish with the basil strips.

Preparation time: approx. 50 minutes
(excluding standing time)
Per serving: approx. 162 kcal/684 kj,
7 g P, 6 g L, 15 g G

Bavarian Sauerkraut Flan

FOR 24 SERVINGS:

160 ml/5½ fl oz milk

400 g/14 oz plain wheat flour

30 g/1 oz fresh yeast

500 g/1 lb 2 oz sauerkraut

80 ml/2¾ fl oz stock

Freshly ground pepper

1 tsp caraway seeds

2 cl/½ tsp wheat beer
(Bavarian if available)

60 g/2 oz butter

1 tsp sugar

A pinch of salt

2 eggs

1 egg yolk

300 g/10½ oz gammon

200 g/7 oz sour cream

150 g/5 oz grated Gruyére
(Swiss cheese)

1 bunch of parsley

1. Heat the milk in a saucepan. Sift the flour into a bowl, make a hollow in the middle and crumble the yeast into it. Pour the milk over it. Knead everything together and leave to rise in a warm place for approx. 20 minutes.

2. Put the sauerkraut in a saucepan with the stock and stir in the pepper, caraway seeds and beer. Heat up and simmer for approx. 8 minutes.

3. Knead the butter, sugar, salt, egg and egg yolk into the dough. Roll the dough into a ball, cover and leave to stand until it has doubled in size.

4. Preheat the oven to 200 °C/ 390 °F/gas mark 6. Slice the gammon into strips. Roll the dough onto a flour-covered working surface and place on a grease-proof paper covered baking tray.

5. Spread the sauerkraut onto the dough. Mix the sour cream with the rest of the eggs and brush onto the sauerkraut. Cover with the gammon and sprinkle the cheese on top.

6. Place on the middle shelf of the oven and bake for approx. 25 minutes.

7. Wash and dry the parsley and then chop it up finely. Sprinkle over the Bavarian sauerkraut flan and serve.

Preparation time: approx. 50 minutes
(excluding standing time)
Per serving: approx. 168 kcal/708 kj,
7 g P, 9 g L, 11 g G

Roquefort Pear Flan

FOR 24 SERVINGS:

300 g/10½ oz plain wheat flour

200 g/7 oz butter, chopped

Salt

A pinch of lemon rind of 1 untreated lemon

1 egg

3 shallots

4 pears

2 tbsp lemon juice

2 tbsp lard

Freshly ground pepper

Nutmeg, freshly ground

250 g/9 oz Roquefort

250 ml/9 fl oz whipping cream

1. Add the flour, butter pieces, salt, lemon rind and egg to a working surface and chop up finely. Knead everything together and roll into a ball, wrap in cling film and leave to stand in a cool place for approx. 1 hour. Preheat the oven to 200 °C/ 390 °F/gas mark 6.

2. Peel the shallots and cut into rings. Peel the pears, cut in half and remove the cores then cut into wedges and sprinkle with the lemon juice.

3. Melt the lard in a pan and gently fry the shallots. Add the pears and fry briefly.

4. Roll the dough out onto a greaseproof paper covered baking tray. Spread the pears onto the dough. Season with the salt, pepper and nutmeg.

5. Stir the cheese and cream together and pour over the flan. Place on the middle shelf of the oven and bake for approx. 25 minutes.

Preparation time: approx. 50 minutes (excluding standing time)
Per serving: approx. 202 kcal/848 kj, 4 g P, 8 g L, 10 g G

Step 2

Rustical Potato Flan

FOR 24 SERVINGS:

160 ml/5½ fl oz milk

400 g/14 oz plain wheat flour

30 g/1 oz fresh yeast

60 g/2 oz butter

1 tsp sugar

Salt

1 egg

1 egg yolk

500 g/1 lb 2 oz hard boiling potatoes

150 g/5 oz tomatoes

Freshly ground pepper

100 g/3½ oz gammon

50 g/1¾ oz corn (tinned)

50 g/1¾ oz peas (tinned)

Paprika powder

350 g/12 oz grated Emmentaler cheese

Herbs, to garnish

1. Heat the milk in a saucepan. Sift the flour into a bowl, make a hollow in the middle and crumble the yeast into it. Pour the milk over it. Knead everything together and leave to rise in a warm place for approx. 20 minutes.

2. Knead the butter, sugar, a pinch of salt, egg and egg yolk into the dough. Roll the dough into a ball, cover and leave to stand until it has doubled in size.

3. While waiting peel the potatoes and cook in salted water for approx. 18 minutes. Drain and cut into slices. Preheat the oven to 180 °C/355 °F/gas mark 4.

4. Trim, wash and half the tomatoes, and then liquidise them with a hand-blender, adding salt and pepper to taste.

5. Cut the gammon into slices. Drain the corn and peas.

6. Cover a baking tray with greaseproof paper and roll the dough onto it. Brush the puréed tomato onto it. Cover with the potato slices, ham, corn and peas. Season with salt, pepper and paprika powder to taste. Sprinkle over with the cheese. Place on the middle shelf of the oven and bake for approx. 30 minutes.

Preparation time: approx. 50 minutes (excluding standing time)
Per serving: approx. 188 kcal/793 kj, 8 g P, 8 g L, 16 g G

Danish Salmon Flan

FOR 24 SERVINGS:

300 g/10½ oz quark
8 tbsp oil
2 eggs
400 g/14 oz flour
½ tsp baking powder
4 tbsp milk
500 g/1 lb 2 oz celery sticks
1 tbsp olive oil
1 clove of garlic
400 g/14 oz salmon fillet
3 tbsp lemon juice
Salt
Freshly ground pepper
3 anchovies (preserved)
250 g/9 oz cream cheese
100 ml/3½ fl oz vegetable stock
Lemon pepper

1. Drain the quark through a sieve, pressing gently to rid excess liquid.

2. Mix the quark with the oil, eggs, flour, baking powder and milk and knead to a smooth dough.

3. Cover a baking tray with grease-proof paper and roll the dough onto it.

4. Trim, wash and dry the celery and chop into small pieces. Heat up the oil in pan and gently fry the celery. Peel the clove of garlic and press it into the celery.

5. Wash the salmon fillets, dry and cut into cubes. Sprinkle with the lemon juice and add to the vegetables. Leave to draw for approx. 10 minutes adding salt and pepper to taste. Preheat the oven to 180 °C/355 °F/gas mark 4.

6. Spread the fish and celery mix onto the dough. Rinse the anchovies with cold water, cut into small pieces and add to the top of the flan.

7. Stir the cream cheese into the vegetable stock and season with some salt and lemon pepper.

8. Spread the cheese over the top of the fish and vegetables and then place on the middle shelf of the oven and bake for approx. 20 minutes.

Preparation time: approx. 50 minutes
(excluding standing time)
Per serving: approx. 177 kcal/746 kj,
8 g P, 9 g L, 11 g G

Goose Flan

FOR 24 SERVINGS:

300 g/10¹/₂ oz plain wheat flour
200 g/7 oz butter, chopped
Salt
1 egg
150 g/5 oz red onions
450 g/1 lb red cabbage with apples (preserved)
150 g/5 oz smoked breast of goose
2 tbsp oil
Freshly ground pepper
50 ml/1³/₄ fl oz cream
100 g/3¹/₂ oz grated Pecorino cheese

1. Add the flour, butter pieces, salt, and egg to a working surface and chop up finely. Knead everything together and roll into a ball, wrap in cling film and leave to stand in a cool place for approx.

1 hour. Preheat the oven to 200 °C/ 390 °F/gas mark 6.

2. Peel the onions and cut into rings. Drain the cabbage. Cut the goose meat into strips. Heat the oil in saucepan and gently fry the onions then add the goose and red cabbage.

3. Roll the dough out onto a greaseproof paper covered baking tray. Spread the meat cabbage mix onto the dough. Season with the salt, and pepper.

4. Dribble the cream over the ingredients and sprinkle the cheese on top. Place on the middle shelf of the oven and bake for 30 minutes.

Preparation time: approx. 50 minutes (excluding standing time)
Per serving: approx. 161 kcal/676 kj, 4 g P, 11 g L, 9 g G

Focaccia "Alfredo"

FOR 24 SERVINGS:

160 ml/5¹/₂ fl oz milk
400 g/14 oz plain wheat flour
30 g/1 oz fresh yeast
60 g/2 oz butter
1 tsp sugar
A pinch of salt
1 egg
1 egg yolk
300 g/10¹/₂ oz red onions
200 g/7 oz green olives
100 g/3¹/₂ oz salami

100 g/3¹/₂ oz small mushrooms

80 g/2³/₄ oz seasoned tomato purée

¹/₂ tsp dried oregano

2 cloves of garlic

1 bunch of basil

1. Heat the milk in a saucepan. Sift the flour into a bowl, make a hollow in the middle and crumble the yeast into it. Pour the milk over it. Knead everything together and leave to rise in a warm place for approx. 20 minutes.

2. Knead the butter, sugar, salt, egg and egg yolk into the dough. Roll the dough into a ball, cover and leave to stand until it has doubled in size.

3. Peel the onions and cut into rings. Drain the olives. Chop the salami into cubes. Wash, dry and cut the mushrooms in half. Preheat the oven to 200 °C/390 °F/ gas mark 6.

4. Cover a baking tray with greaseproof paper and roll the dough onto it. Brush the tomato purée onto the dough. Spread the ingredients over the tomato mix and sprinkle over with the oregano. Peel the garlic and press on to the topping. Wash and dry the basil and cut into strips.

5. Place on the middle shelf of the oven and bake for approx. 25 minutes. Before serving garnish with the basil strips.

Preparation time: approx. 50 minutes (excluding standing time)
Per serving: approx. 123 kcal/520 kj, 4 g P, 6 g L, 13 g G

Step 4

Cheese and Onion Flan

FOR 24 SERVINGS:

160 ml/5½ fl oz milk

400 g/14 oz plain wheat flour

30 g/1 oz fresh yeast

60 g/2 oz butter

1 tsp sugar

A pinch of salt

1 egg

1 egg yolk

700 g/1 lb 9 oz shallots

700 g/1 lb 9 oz Emmentaler cheese

Pepper

A pinch of cumin powder

Herbs, to decorate

1. Heat the milk in a saucepan. Sift the flour into a bowl, make a hollow in the middle and crumble the yeast into it. Pour the milk over it. Knead everything together and leave to rise in a warm place for approx. 20 minutes.

2. Knead the butter, sugar, salt, egg and egg yolk into the dough. Roll the dough into a ball, cover and leave to stand until it has doubled in size.

3. Peel the shallots and cut into cubes. Grate the cheese. Add the onions and cheese to a bowl stirring together and seasoning with salt, pepper and cumin powder. Preheat the oven to 200 °C/390 °F/gas mark 6.

4. Cover a baking tray with greaseproof paper and roll the dough onto it. Cover with the cheese and onion mix. Place on the middle shelf of the oven and bake for approx. 25 minutes.

Before serving garnish with the herbs.

Preparation time: approx. 50 minutes (excluding standing time)
Per serving: approx. 213 kcal/898 kj, 10 g P, 10 g L, 16 g G

Step 3

148

Tomato Flan

FOR 24 SERVINGS:

300 g/10¹/₂oz plain wheat flour

200 g/7 oz chopped butter

A pinch of salt

A pinch of grated lemon rind

1 egg

700 g/1 lb 9 oz plum tomatoes

250 g/9 oz goats milk cheese

3 tbsp capers

3 spring onions

Salt

Freshly ground pepper

1 bunch of rosemary

3 cloves of garlic

100 g/3¹/₂ oz Gruyère cheese, thinly sliced

1. Add the flour, butter pieces, salt, and egg to a working surface and chop up finely. Knead everything together and roll into a ball, wrap in cling film and leave to stand in a cool place for approx. 1 hour. Preheat the oven to 200 °C/ 390 °F/gas mark 6.

2. Trim and wash the tomatoes and cut into slices. Stir together the capers and goats milk cheese. Trim and wash the spring onions and chop into rings and fold into the cheese and capers.

3. Roll the dough out onto a greaseproof paper covered baking tray. Cover the dough with the cheese. Top with the tomato slices overlapping them likes roof tiles. Season with the salt and pepper.

4. Wash and dry the rosemary and pull off the needles. Peel the cloves of garlic and cut into thin slices.

5. Sprinkle the tomatoes with the rosemary and garlic and top off with the Gruyère. Place on the middle shelf of the oven and bake for approx. 25 minutes.

Preparation time: approx. 50 minutes (excluding standing time)
Per serving: approx. 160 kcal/674 kj, 4 g P, 10 g L, 10 g G

Paprika Flan

FOR 24 SERVINGS:

160 ml/5½ fl oz milk

400 g/14 oz plain wholemeal wheat flour

30 g/1 oz fresh yeast

60 g/2 oz butter

40 g/1½ oz sugar

Salt

1 egg

1 egg yolk

200 g/7 oz red peppers

200 g/7 oz yellow peppers

2 tbsp herbed butter

2 cloves of garlic

80 g/2¾ oz black olives

3 eggs

100 g/3½ oz grated Emmentaler cheese

1. Heat the milk in a saucepan. Sift the flour into a bowl, make a hollow in the middle and crumble the yeast into it. Pour the milk over it. Knead everything together and leave to rise in a warm place for approx. 20 minutes.

2. Knead the butter, sugar, salt, egg and egg yolk into the dough. Roll the dough into a ball, cover and leave to stand until it has doubled in size.

3. Preheat the oven to 200 °C/ 390 °F/gas mark 6. Trim and wash the peppers and cut into strips. Melt the butter in a pan and gently fry the peppers. Press the garlic and add. Drain the olives and add.

4. Cover a baking tray with greaseproof paper and roll the dough onto it. Cover with the pepper mix. Beat the eggs and the cheese and salt to taste. Pour over the pepper topping. Place on the middle shelf of the oven and bake for approx. 25 minutes.

Preparation time: approx. 50 minutes
(excluding standing time)
Per serving: approx. 144 kcal/605 kj,
5 g P, 6 g L, 14 g G

Mini "Flores" Pizzas

FOR 24 PIZZAS:

160 ml/5½ fl oz milk

400 g/14 oz plain wholemeal wheat flour

30 g/1 oz fresh yeast

60 g/2 oz butter

40 g/1½ oz sugar

Salt

1 egg

1 egg yolk

400 g/14 oz plum tomatoes

300 g/10½ oz goats milk cheese

1 bunch of basil

Pepper

4 tbsp olive oil

1. Heat the milk in a saucepan. Sift the flour into a bowl, make a hollow in the middle and crumble the yeast into it. Pour the milk over it. Knead everything together and leave to rise in a warm place for approx. 20 minutes.

2. Knead the butter, sugar, salt, egg and egg yolk into the dough.

Roll the dough into a ball, cover and leave to stand until it has doubled in size.

3. Preheat the oven to 200 °C/ 390 °F/gas mark 6. Trim and wash the peppers and cut into strips. Wash the tomatoes and chop into cubes. Cut the goats cheese into slices. Wash the basil and cut into strips.

4. Roll out the dough on a flour-covered working surface and into a baguette sized length. Cut into slices and roll into small balls. Cut and cross into the balls. Place on a greaseproof paper covered baking tray. Add the tomato cubes to each mini pizza and sprinkle with cheese. Season with the basil, salt and pepper and some drops of olive oil. Place on the middle shelf of the oven and bake for approx. 15 minutes.

Preparation time: approx. 50 minutes (excluding standing time)
Per serving: approx. 436 kcal/1948 kj, 17 g P, 23 g L, 40 g G

Step 1

Step 3

Delicate Asparagus Slices

FOR 24 SERVINGS:

300 g/10^1/$_2$ oz quark

8 tbsp oil

5 eggs

400 g/14 oz flour

^{1}/$_2$ tsp baking powder

4 tbsp milk

1 kg/2 lbs 3 oz green asparagus

Salt

250 g/9 oz yoghurt

1 egg white

3 tbsp whipping cream

Freshly ground pepper

250 g/9 oz North Sea prawns

2 tbsp Aquavit liqueur

Herbs, to garnish

1. Drain the quark through a sieve, pressing down gently to rid excess liquid.

2. Mix the quark with the oil, 2 eggs, flour, baking powder and milk and knead into a smooth dough.

3. Roll onto a greaseproof paper covered baking tray.

4. Wash the asparagus, and trim off the lower ends. Cook in a saucepan of lightly salted water for approx. 10 minutes.

5. While waiting stir together the yoghurt, the remaining eggs, egg white and cream. Season with salt and pepper. Stir in the prawns and Aquavit. Preheat the oven to 180 °C/355 °F/gas mark 4.

6. Drain the asparagus and spread over the dough.

7. Cover the asparagus with the yoghurt mix and then place on the middle shelf of the oven and bake for approx. 20 minutes. Garnish with the herbs and dribble with lemon to taste and then serve.

Preparation time: approx. 45 min
Per serving: approx. 154 kcal/649 kj,
7 g P, 7 g L, 12 g G

Marions Green Cabbage Flan

FOR 24 SERVINGS:

160 ml/5¹/₂ fl oz milk

400 g/14 oz plain wheat flour

30 g/1 oz fresh yeast

60 g/2 oz butter

1 tsp sugar

A pinch of salt

1 egg

1 egg yolk

800 g/1 lb 12 oz green cabbage

500 ml vegetable stock

Salt, freshly ground pepper

400 g/14 oz turkey breast fillets

2 tbsp butter

250 g/9 oz goats milk cheese

1. Heat the milk in a saucepan. Sift the flour into a bowl, make a hollow in the middle and crumble the yeast into it. Pour the milk over it. Knead everything together and leave to rise in a warm place for approx. 20 minutes.

2. Knead the butter, sugar, salt, egg and egg yolk into the dough. Roll the dough into a ball, cover and leave to stand until it has doubled in size.

3. Trim and wash the green cabbage and cut into small pieces. Add to the vegetable stock, heat up and cook for 5 minutes. Season with salt and pepper.

4. Wash the meat and dab it dry and then cut into slices. Season with salt and pepper. Melt the butter in a frying pan and fry the meat until cooked through. Drain the cabbage, add to the meat and fry briefly.

5. Preheat the oven to 200 °C/ 390 °F/gas mark 6. Roll out the dough on a flour-covered working surface and put on a prepared baking tray. Spread the meat and cabbage over the dough. Chop the cheese into small pieces and sprinkle over the top.

6. Place on the middle shelf of the oven and bake for aprox. 30 minutes.

Preparation time: approx. 50 minutes
(excluding standing time)
Per serving: approx. 156 kcal/659 kj,
10 g P, 6 g L, 12 g G

Spinach Flan

For 24 servings:

160 ml/5½ fl oz milk

400 g/14 oz plain wheat flour

30 g/1 oz fresh yeast

60 g/2 oz butter

1 tsp sugar

Salt

1 egg

1 egg yolk

400 g/14 oz leaf spinach

400 g/14 oz tomatoes

200 g/7 oz smoked streaky bacon

3 onions

2 tbsp herbed butter

Salt

Freshly ground pepper

Paprika powder

2 cloves of garlic

200 g/7 oz grated Gruyère cheese

1. Heat the milk in a saucepan. Sift the flour into a bowl, make a hollow in the middle and crumble the yeast into it. Pour the milk over it. Knead everything together and leave to rise in a warm place for approx. 20 minutes.

2. Knead the butter, sugar, a pinch of salt, egg and egg yolk into the dough. Roll the dough into a ball, cover and leave to stand until it has doubled in size. Preheat the oven to 180 °C/355 °F/gas mark 4.

3. Wash and dry the spinach. Wash and dry the tomatoes and slice into thin wedges. Cut the bacon into thin strips. Peel the onions and cut into rings.

4. Melt the herbed butter in a frying pan and briefly fry the ingredients. Season well with the salt, pepper and paprika powder.

5. Roll out the dough onto a greaseproof paper covered baking tray and cover with the vegetables. Peel the two cloves of garlic and press them over the vegetables. Sprinkle the cheese on top and place on the middle shelf of the oven and bake for approx. 25 minutes.

Preparation time: approx. 50 minutes (excluding standing time)
Per serving: approx. 173 kcal/730 kj, 7 g P, 9 g L, 13 g G

Swabian Mushroom Pizza

For 24 servings:

160 ml/5½ fl oz milk

400 g/14 oz plain wheat flour

30 g/1 oz fresh yeast

60 g/2 oz butter

1 tsp sugar

A pinch of salt

1 egg

1 egg yolk

3 onions

250 g/9 oz mushrooms

1 tbsp oil
375 g/13 oz sausages
50 g/1¾ oz gammon, cut into strips
250 g/9 oz red and green bell peppers, cut into strips
Salt
Freshly ground pepper
Chilli powder
200 g/7 oz plum tomatoes
200 g/7 oz Bavarian blue cheese

1. Heat the milk in a saucepan. Sift the flour into a bowl, make a hollow in the middle and crumble the yeast into it. Pour the milk over it. Knead everything together and leave to rise in a warm place for approx. 20 minutes.

2. Knead the butter, sugar, salt, egg and egg yolk into the dough.

Roll the dough into a ball, cover and leave to stand until it has doubled in size.

3. Peel the onions and slice into rings. Trim and wash the mushrooms and chop into pieces. Heat the oil in a pan and gently fry the onions and then mushrooms. Add the sausages, ham and peppers and continue to fry. Season with salt and pepper and chilli powder. Preheat the oven to 200 °C/390 °F/ gas mark 6.

4. Roll out the dough on a greaseproof paper covered baking tray and cover with the fried ingredients. Trim and wash the tomatoes and chop into eighths, slice the cheese and sprinkle both over the pizza.

Place on the middle shelf of the oven and bake for approx. 15 minutes.

Preparation time: approx. 50 minutes (excluding standing time)
Per serving: approx. 190 kcal/799 kj, 8 g P, 10 g L, 13 g G

Step 3

155

Green Corn Bread Rolls

FOR 24 SERVINGS:

160 ml/5½ fl oz milk

400 g/14 oz rye flour

30 g/1 oz fresh yeast

60 g/2 oz butter

40 g/1½ oz sugar

A pinch of salt

1 egg

1 egg yolk

1 tsp caraway seeds

1 tsp linseeds

1 tsp sunflower seeds

100 g/3½ oz mixed herbs
(frozen or fresh)

1. Heat the milk in a saucepan. Sift the flour into a bowl, make a hollow in the middle and crumble the yeast into it. Pour the milk over it. Knead everything together and leave to rise in a warm place for approx. 20 minutes.

2. Knead the butter, sugar, salt, egg and egg yolk into the dough. Roll the dough into a ball, cover and leave to stand until it has doubled in size.

3. Preheat the oven to 200 °C/ 390 °F/gas mark 6. Knead the caraway seeds, linseeds and sunflower seeds, the mixed herbs into the dough. Leave to rise for about another 5 minutes.

4. Separate the dough into segments and make small long loaves out of them, scoring diagonally across the top with a knife. Place on a greaseproof paper covered baking tray and on the middle shelf of the oven and bake for approx. 30 minutes.

Preparation time: approx. 50 minutes
(sans temps de repos)
Per serving: approx. 97 kcal/407 kj,
2 g P, 3 g L, 13 g G

Egg and Vegetable Flan

FOR 24 SERVINGS:

160 ml/5½ fl oz milk

400 g/14 oz plain wheat flour

30 g/1 oz fresh yeast

60 g/2 oz butter

40 g/1½ oz sugar

A pinch of salt

1 egg

1 egg yolk

50 g/1¾ oz ketchup

5 cherry tomatoes

250 g/9 oz pointed cabbage

1 onion

2 cloves of garlic

Salt

Freshly ground pepper

200 g/7 oz mozzarella slices

1 bunch of parsley

1. Heat the milk in a saucepan. Sift the flour into a bowl, make a hollow in the middle and crumble the yeast into it. Pour the milk over it. Knead everything together and leave to rise in a warm place for approx. 20 minutes.

2. Knead the butter, sugar, salt, egg and egg yolk into the dough. Roll the dough into a ball, cover and leave to stand until it has doubled in size.

3. Preheat the oven to 200 °C/ 390 °F/gas mark 6. Roll the dough out onto a flour-covered working surface and place on a grease-proof paper covered baking tray. Spread the ketchup onto the dough.

4. Wash and dry the tomatoes and then slice into halves. Wash and dry the cabbage and cut into strips. Peel the onion and chop into cubes.

5. Peel the garlic and press. Cover the flan with all the prepared vegetables. Place on the middle shelf of the oven and bake for approx. 25 minutes. Trim and wash the parsley, chop it up finely garnish the ready baked flan and then serve.

Preparation time: approx. 50 minutes (excluding standing time)
Per serving: approx. 125 kcal/525 kj, 4 g P, 5 g L, 13 g G

Prawn and Vegetable Quiche

FOR 24 SERVINGS:

300 g/10½ oz quark

8 tbsp oil

5 eggs

400 g/14 oz flour

½ tsp baking powder

4 tbsp milk

Butter, to grease the quiche dish

300 g/10½ oz courgettes

150 g/5 oz spring onions

200 g/7 oz North Sea prawns

2 tbsp oil

1 small chilli pepper

2 cloves of garlic

Salt

Freshly ground pepper

Mixed herbs, to garnish

1. Drain the quark through a sieve, pressing down gently to rid excess liquid.

2. Mix the quark with the oil, 2 eggs, flour, baking powder and milk and knead to a smooth dough.

3. Roll the dough out onto a flour-covered working surface. Grease a 24 cm/9½ in quiche dish and line it with the dough.

4. Trim and wash the courgettes and cut into strips. Trim and wash the spring onions and cut into rings. Wash the North Sea prawns. Preheat the oven to 180 °C/355 °F/ gas mark 4.

5. Heat the oil in a pan and fry the vegetables in it gently. Add the prawns. Wash the chilli peppers and chop up finely. Peel the garlic and press into the vegetables. Add the chilli while stirring and season with salt and pepper.

6. Turn the vegetable fish mix into the quiche dish. Beat the remaining eggs adding salt and pour over everything.

7. Place on the middle shelf of the oven and bake for approx. 25 minutes. Serve garnished with some mixed herbs.

Preparation time: approx. 45 minutes
Per serving: approx. 81 kcal/341 kj,
4 g P, 5 g L, 1 g G

Cheesey Herb Sticks

FOR 24 STICKS:

200 g/7 oz flaky pastry

2 eggs

200 g/7 oz grated Emmentaler cheese

1 bunch of basil

Salt

Freshly ground pepper

paprika powder

Sesame seeds, to garnish

Decorating sugar

1. Roll the flaky pastry onto a flour-covered working surface and brush with a beaten egg.

2. Mix the cheese and remaining eggs in a bowl. Wash and dry the basil and cut into strips. Fold into the cheese mix and season with salt, pepper and paprika powder.

3. Preheat the oven to 200 °C/ 390 °F/gas mark 6. Cut the pastry into long strips. Brush half of the strips with the cheese mix and place the other strips on top pressing down.

4. Twist the strips within themselves and place onto a grease-proof paper covered baking tray. Sprinkle with the sesame seeds

and decorating sugar. Place on the middle shelf of the oven and bake for approx. 10 minutes.

Preparation time: approx. 50 minutes
Per serving: approx. 223 kcal/936 kj,
4 g P, 10 g L, 12 g G

Step 1

Index of Recipes